W9-CWR-348

Dear Frances . . .

Dear Frances...

I have a problem.

Can you help me?

By
FRANCES NORDLAND

MOODY PRESS
CHICAGO

TO
Chauncey,
whose love and encouragement
have meant so much to me

Contents

Preface

"So women actually write to you about the problems I have heard you present on the air!" This remark was made by a visitor to the studios of the Moody Bible Institute in Chicago after she saw the papers in my hands following a recording session. I replied, "Yes," and added: "I deal with some problems that may seem unreal, but I am convinced they are not unique. One woman's problem usually represents a similar problem in the lives of other women."

It's easy for a woman to think that no one else has a problem like hers. However, though each of us is unique as an individual, created by God with distinct differences, yet we have many things in common.

We all experience trials. The apostle Paul wrote, "There hath no temptation [trial] taken you but such as is common to man" (1 Corinthians 10:13). Those who experience trials often view them as problems. Kenneth Taylor uses the word *problems* in his paraphrase of 1 Corinthians 10:13: "remember this—the wrong desires that come into your life aren't anything new and different. Many others have faced exactly the same problems before you. And no temptation is irresistible. You can trust God to keep the temptation from becoming so strong that you can't stand up against it, for he has promised this and will do what he says. He will show you how to escape temptation's power so that you can bear up patiently against it." (TLB[1]).

When temptations are presented to a Christian to think

---

1. *The Living Bible* (Wheaton, Ill.: Tyndale, 1971).

or act in ways that are specifically referred to in the Bible as sinful, there is no question about what God wants him to do. He must resist the temptation or flee from it. And he can learn from the Bible the spiritual resources God has made available to His children so that they can escape temptation's power.

But there are some situations that confront Christians about which the Bible doesn't speak specifically. When this is so, Christians often find help in seeking counsel from other Christians. We read in the book of Proverbs, "He that hearkeneth unto counsel is wise" (12:15). Often a counselor, because he isn't emotionally involved in the situation, can look at a problem more objectively than the person facing the problem can.

As I have given answers to the problems included in this book, I have endeavored to avoid triteness. I have tried to "think through" the problems in the light of the principles for living taught in the Bible. In addition, I have brought to the problems the insight gained from my experiences as a pastor's wife for thirty years, a mother, a widow, and a partner in a very happy second marriage after five years of widowhood. Needless to say, I have also learned much from the vast amount of reading required to prepare my radio programs and from personal contacts with women whom I have met in my personal appearances.

I have learned that not all problems have easy solutions. Indeed, some Christians may find no solutions to some of their problems during their lifetime. But even though they do not now understand why they must endure certain trials and why some problems remain unsolved, some day they will understand. The apostle Paul said, as paraphrased in *The Living Bible,* "Now all that I know is hazy and blurred, but then I will see everything clearly, just as God sees into my heart right now" (1 Corinthians 13:12).

It is my hope that the answers given to the questions

presented in this book will help some individuals to find solutions—or partial solutions—for their problems, or to appropriate God's all-sufficient grace for living with their problems. However, before an individual resigns himself to living with the problem, he ought to explore the possibilities of change. When I say this, I am thinking of the familiar prayer that goes like this:

> God, grant me the serenity to accept the things I cannot change, courage to change the things I can, and wisdom to know the difference.

Of course, each person must consider that he might be part of the problem. As he accepts strength from God to make changes in his life the problem may be eliminated or—if not eliminated—eased. But if the second person involved in a problem doesn't respond to any changes made in the conduct and attitudes of the first person, then he must accept God's grace to live with the problem.

While trials, or problems, are "common" to man, those who have become members of the family of God through personal faith in Jesus Christ as their Saviour have in common the spiritual resources God has made available to *all* His children. Among the resources they share are these:

1. The Bible, God's Word, which is the Christian's spiritual food. In the Bible we find precious promises of God (2 Peter 1:4), including promises of God's abundant grace (2 Corinthians 9:8), of divine strength (2 Corinthians 12:9; Philippians 4:13), and of the supply of every need (Philippians 4:19), including wisdom (James 1:5).

2. The indwelling presence of the Holy Spirit, who is the Christian's teacher and faithful guide. He will instruct Christians in ways to apply biblical principles to everyday living.

Yes, there are problems in life, but the Christian can

11

grow by thinking through and working through his problems with God.

"Dear brothers, is your life full of difficulties and temptations? Then be happy, for when the way is rough, your patience has a chance to grow. So let it grow, and don't try to squirm out of your problems. For when your patience is finally in full bloom, then you will be ready for anything, strong in character, full and complete" (James 1:2-4 TLB).

In My Daily Life

Dear Frances,

I am a young mother with a very active two-year-old son, and I am expecting another child.

As I look back on the last couple of years I see that my prayer life has slipped a bit. How does a Christian mother get back on the track, so to speak, with such a terribly full home life?

It's natural for a young mother to become absorbed in taking care of her new baby. And it's easy to neglect personal Bible reading and prayer during the period when she is learning how to adjust her home life to the unfamiliar tasks connected with meeting the requirements of her baby. She experiences that homemaking and baby care fill most of the hours of her day. Recently I read about some kind of law that could be applied to homemakers: "There's always enough work to fill up the time that is available."

What's a young mother to do? The solution, it seems to me, is to subtract ten or fifteen minutes from the time available for your housework and devote that time to Bible reading and prayer. Make up your mind to do it. God has given you a will that you can use to will to do what you believe to be His will for you.

I am aware that many young mothers are tired all the time. Some doctors tell such mothers that they have too many things to do in the time available to them. Therefore they ought to make up their minds that they won't be able

13

to earn the title "Perfect Housekeeper" during the period when their children are small. They must plan on leaving some things undone. I might add that many a husband would rather put up with less-than-perfect housekeeping in order to have a less tired wife. Your disposition will improve if you don't push yourself too hard during this particular period in your life.

I recognize that many homemaking duties seem urgent to you. But, as someone has said, we must learn to make a distinction between what is urgent and what is important. Your spiritual well-being and progress in maturing as a Christian are important. Therefore you should make it a point of high priority to read the Bible and pray every day, if possible.

If you find you have to make a choice between Bible reading and prayer, I would suggest that you read the Bible, for this is the Christian's spiritual food. You can pray to God while you are busy with various tasks around the home. Someone has called this "praying on the run," but it's better than not praying at all. Besides, if we thought of prayer as acceptable to God only when we are on our knees, how then could we fulfill the command found in 1 Thessalonians 5:17: "Pray without ceasing"?

Dear Frances,
Recently I read a book in which the author said, "God doesn't want your every waking minute because He realizes there are other things one has to do."
How do you evaluate this statement?

It seems to me that the author probably was thinking of the unrealistic concept held by some Christians of consciously living every moment of the day in God's presence and constantly thinking about Him.

God knows what our duties in life are. Sometimes they

are such that we must concentrate our thoughts completely on the work at hand. And we glorify God by striving for excellence, by doing a good job no matter what the task. But when we are released from the need for concentration, we can turn our thoughts Godward and acknowledge His presence by praying quietly, "Thank You, Lord, for helping me" or "Thank You for Your presence."

We can begin each day with God with a prayer that includes committing the events of our day to Him and asking for His guidance and strength. We can go into our day with the certainty that our Father will be with us and help us even when we are not thinking about Him and talking to Him.

Dear Frances,

I have been praying for some time about some things that mean much to me: My husband's salvation; finances for the college education of our three children (twenty-one, nineteen, and seventeen) since my husband's salary is modest; my children's spiritual needs; and my desire to lose weight. I weigh three hundred pounds, and doctors have found that I only require eight hundred calories a day to exist.

When do prayers become vain repetitions?

The expression "vain repetitions" was used by the Lord Jesus in His Sermon on the Mount. The expression occurs in a context where He had been criticizing individuals whom He described as hypocrites. These gave alms in such a way that they called attention to their acts of giving, and they prayed in public (in synagogues and on street corners) in order to be seen of men. Then Jesus said, "But thou, when thou prayest, enter into thy closet, and when thou hast shut thy door, pray to thy Father which is in secret; and thy Father which seeth in secret shall reward thee openly. But when ye pray, use not vain repetitions, as the heathen do: for they think that they shall be heard for their much speaking" (Matthew 6:6-7).

I think the expression "vain repetitions" may be applied to repetition of set prayers (read, or recited after learning them by rote) as practiced in some liturgical churches. It might also be applied to the practice of Lamaist Buddhists who write out a prayer and put it on a prayer wheel or in a drum to turn round and round. This would be mechanical repetition.

The Living New Testament's rendering of Matthew 6:7-8 goes this way: "Don't recite the same prayer over and over as the heathen do, who think prayers are answered only by repeating them again and again. Remember, your Father knows exactly what you need even before you ask Him!"

Evidently the motive for heathen repeating their prayers again and again was this: They thought the frequency of their repetition would be the reason their prayers would be answered.

You might ask, "Why should we pray to God about any of our needs, since He knows before we begin praying what our needs are?" The answer to that question is this: By praying to God we acknowledge that He is the Giver of every good gift and we recognize that He is our loving heavenly Father, deeply interested in those who are His children. In praying about our needs, we honor Him. Also when we pour out our hearts before Him, we are helped emotionally. The pressures don't seem quite so great when we express how we feel to One who loves us, who cares for us, and who can do something—and *will* do something—about our needs.

When we have such an attitude, we can come to the Lord again and again without our prayers becoming vain repetitions. The person who makes vain repetitions is the one who feels that he will get an answer from God just because he has prayed so often. But we don't get answers from God because we deserve them. God answers the prayers of His children because they pray in the name of Jesus. Christians should realize that they have no merit of their own that gives them a right to make claims on God. Our merit before God is Jesus Christ, who alone is our righteousness. Our faith in Jesus Christ as our Saviour is the basis of our acceptance before God.

Jesus did teach that men should always pray and not faint (or give up), and this teaching would seem to warrant our coming to God again and again with specific petitions. He illustrated this aspect of prayer by telling about a widow who was taken advantage of by a person designated as her "adversary." Jesus' story (found in Luke 18:1-5) told how she went to a judge and asked him to avenge her of her adversary. In other words, this woman, who had no husband to defend her rights, was demanding justice against a man who had harmed her. But the judge to whom she came was described as one who did not fear God, nor did he care what men thought of him. For a while he refused to listen to her appeals, but finally he said to himself, "Even though I don't fear God or care what people think, I'll have to see that this widow gets just treatment, or she'll keep coming until she wears me out." In the Berkeley Version the words translated in King James Version, "lest . . . she weary me" are rendered "so she may not . . . wear me down," with this footnote, "literally, beat me black and blue."

What a picture this story gives of perseverance—a persistence that will not take no for an answer.

Following this story Jesus presented a contrast between the character of the unjust judge and the character of God, who is righteous. Those who are God's children know that He is not only righteous but also very loving and generous. When we come to Him with specific petitions, He will

17

answer us in His own time, determined by His sovereign will and His infinite wisdom.

When we come to God again and again with specific requests, this doesn't indicate that we doubt that He has heard us. Instead, we are reminding Him of our needs, just talking over with Him the requests that are close to our hearts. We are fully persuaded that what matters to us matters to Him.

Of course, there may come a time when you will receive an inner conviction that you should no longer pray about a certain matter. The experience of the apostle Paul illustrates what I mean. After he had begged God, three different times, to remove his thorn in the flesh, he accepted what God said to him. God said no, but along with the no, God gave a wonderful promise: "My grace is sufficient for thee: for my strength is made perfect in weakness" (2 Corinthians 12:9).

I might also mention that in the Garden of Gethsemane Jesus prayed three times, "Father, if it be possible, let this cup pass from me," each time adding, "Not my will but thine be done."

When you pray about subjects such as you have mentioned, you are doing what the apostle Paul told the Christians at Philippi to do: "Be careful [anxious] for nothing; but in every thing by prayer and supplication with thanksgiving let your requests be made known unto God." When Paul wrote those words, as recorded in Philippians 4:6, he didn't promise that positive answers would come right away. If you have to wait for an answer to your prayers, you can experience the fulfilling of the promise that went along with Paul's command to pray about everything: "And the peace of God, which passeth all understanding, shall keep your hearts and minds through Christ Jesus" (Philippians 4:7).

You say that you are praying about your excess weight.

This is a legitimate concern to present to God in prayer. However, we cannot expect God to do for us what we can— and must—do for ourselves. As you acknowledge your "weakness" as far as willpower is concerned (or perhaps we ought to say, as far as "won't power" is concerned), you can ask God to strengthen your will to make choices in harmony with what you believe to be His will for you.

Some individuals who have written to me about their difficulties in losing weight say that they definitely feel it is God's will for them to lose weight. Well, if a person feels that way, then he can rely on God's help in attaining his goal of reaching a normal weight and then maintaining it. But achieving this will require, in some cases, more than a definite decision and prayer for God's aid. You may need a thorough physical examination by a doctor to determine if there is an unusual factor which must be taken into account in planning a weight reduction program for you. However, I have read that doctors say that in perhaps ninety-five percent of cases what is needed is willpower— the ability to cut down on one's intake of food.

Dear Frances,

My husband and I both have problems.

I feel these problems are with us because we haven't been fully yielded to Jesus Christ. With my husband this lack of yieldedness manifests itself in his being unable to give up smoking, although he knows he should.

With me, my lack of yieldedness is shown in rebellion. I initiated a situation that got me into a difficult relationship with some individuals. I feel bitterness toward them, and I dislike them. This situation fills my thought life, as I am so frequently reminded of the persons concerned because I see them frequently. The only way out is victory through Christ. Going far enough away would help some, but the Lord has not seen fit to include such a move in His will for us.

Can you help us?

I think it's much easier to recognize our lack of yieldedness to God than it is to actually yield to God's will for us.

God will not bring us into a yielded state just by saying a magic word. *We* need to use the power of choice with which He has endowed us.

In Romans 6:12-13 the apostle Paul wrote to the Christians at Rome, "Let not sin therefore reign in your mortal body, that ye should obey it in the lusts [or strong desires] thereof. Neither yield ye your members as instruments of unrighteousness unto sin: but yield yourselves unto God, as those that are alive from the dead, and your members as instruments of righteousness unto God." Paul didn't instruct them to *pray* about it; rather he told them what they should *not* do and what they *should* do.

You may be asking, "But what about the power of sin in the life of an individual?" As you read the New Testament, you will learn that the power of sin over the believer in Jesus Christ has been annulled through His death on the cross. That is why Paul said, "Sin shall not have dominion over you" (Romans 6:14). You will also learn that God reckons the believer to have died with Jesus and to have been raised with Him. The believer too is to reckon on his union with Jesus in His death and resurrection as a fact. Such reckoning is an act of faith. We make room for God's power in our lives when we believe what He said, when we act in faith because we believe the facts.

Paul also said, in Philippians 2:12, "Work out your own salvation [deliverance] with fear and trembling." One version translates "with fear and trembling" this way: "with reverence and trepidation"; another translates it: "with reverence and self-distrust"; and still another gives

20

this rendering: "with reverence and awe." As we work out our own deliverance from the habits of sin and from impulses to do what is wrong, we can recognize that it is *God* who works in us "both to *will* and to *do* of his good pleasure." The Berkeley Version translates: "God is the Energizer within you, so as to *will* and to *work* for His delight."

God gave you the gift of salvation when you trusted in Jesus as your Saviour. That was the beginning of new life for you, because you were born into God's family. But then, like a newborn babe, you needed to grow. Growth to maturity in the spiritual life requires your feeding on spiritual food—the Word of God. By reading and studying the Bible you learn God's standards for His children, and, as you seek His guidance, the Holy Spirit who dwells within you will guide you in applying the principles for Christian living that you find in the Bible to particular situations in your life. With knowledge of God's Word and the leading of the Holy Spirit, you should be able to discriminate between good and evil. It is this ability, according to Hebrews 5:14, that is an evidence of maturity. Of course, the ability to discriminate between good and evil implies that you are then responsible to choose the good and reject the evil. In other words, you are responsible for choosing to obey God or to disobey Him.

As you go through life and face situations in which you find a conflict between your will and God's will, and you then choose to do God's will, as far as you know it, you will grow. God will not make these choices for you; *you* must make them; *you* must decide.

However, whenever you discern in yourself an unwillingness to choose God's will, you can pray that God will strengthen your will to *will* His will.

Regarding the thoughts of bitterness and resentment that plague you, I would say this: You *can* control your

21

thoughts. If this were not so, the apostle Paul wouldn't have said, "Think on these things," when he told the Christians at Philippi to think about the things that are true, honest, just, pure, lovely, virtuous, praiseworthy, and of good report (Philippians 4:8). Nor would he have told the Christians at Colosse, "Set your affection [mind] on things above, not on things on the earth." Just as you can turn the dial of your radio or television set to another station in order to change programs, you can, by an act of your will, choose to turn from a "program" of bitter, resentful thinking to the kind of thinking that issues out of love produced by the Holy Spirit.

As I think about your husband's inability to give up smoking, I would point out that in some church groups smoking is not considered a sin and "worldly." Naturally, your husband would feel guilty about smoking if you are members of a church that has adopted the standard of non-smoking for members. Now, every organization has a right to make its own rules about smoking, the use of intoxicating liquors, attending the theater, dancing, playing cards, and so on. If you join an organization that has adopted such standards, I think you should conform to those standards. It's a matter of personal integrity to keep a pledge you make when joining a church or other religious group, or else sever your connection with the organization. This principle would also apply to young people who attend Christian schools with prescribed codes of conduct.

I feel that a Christian who has yielded his body to Jesus Christ, as Paul asked Christians to do (in Romans 12:1-2), would want to abstain from smoking. Since reports from a number of research projects show that cigarette smoking is responsible for the large increase in lung cancer deaths, and since patients with emphysema, ulcers, and coronary diseases are told by their doctors to give up smoking, it seems to me that a Christian would want to abstain from smoking and from any other habit that will adversely affect the health and efficiency of his body. His body belongs to God and is the instrument through which he can serve God in this life.

Since cigarette smoking is an expensive habit, the cost of smoking should be another consideration, especially for those individuals who view the money which comes into their possession as a stewardship for which they are responsible to God.

Motivation is a big factor in giving up any harmful habit. If you do it to please the Lord because you view your body as a temple of the Holy Spirit, you have a strong motivation. If you love the Lord sincerely and deeply, you will choose to deny yourself in order to please Him.

I might add that many of us know by experience how hard it is to give up something that gives us pleasure or affords release from tensions, for most Americans are fighting a battle that someone has called "the battle of the bulge." Overweight, like smoking, is harmful to one's health and a hindrance to maximum efficiency. Of course, I realize some individuals who read this will say, "Now you've left off preaching; you're meddling."

Dear Frances,
I have been talking with a very strong-minded person who will not admit that he could be wrong about a certain matter, even though I can prove to him that he is wrong. How can I get him to face the truth?

You can very seldom convince a person through argument, especially if his emotions are deeply involved. It is impossible to argue with an emotion, and when two contrary emotions meet without the benefit of reason or intelligence, there is bound to be trouble. There is no common wave length by which the two persons involved can communicate.

The longer you continue to argue, the stronger becomes the clash of conflicting feelings, and the gap of hostility is widened.

You might ask yourself, "Why do I want to prove this person wrong?" Perhaps, after thoughtful reflection, you will come to see that your reasons do not spring out of a desire to bring some benefit to that person's life but rather out of a selfish desire to prove that *you* are right.

The other person may want to prove you wrong and himself right for the same reason.

I would advise you to drop the matter if, after one good discussion, you cannot come to an agreement. After all, not all of us need to agree on everything. We will have differences of opinion. However, mature individuals should be able to accept others as persons even if they can't accept their views on some subjects.

A conciliating phrase you may want to try using when involved in discussions is this: "You *may* be right."

With My Young Children

Dear Frances,

I am the mother of a three-year-old boy. I left him with baby-sitters when he was small, but when he got a bit older my husband and I took him with us when we went out, or else we stayed home. I felt it was my responsibility to raise my children, as baby-sitters aren't always as dependable as I would like. Furthermore, the early years of a child are such impressionable years that I felt these were the years I should devote to my son. I realize I may be going way overboard on this.

Now I am wondering how I should go about teaching my son to be a little more independent of me. He is a timid boy and usually doesn't speak to older people. We have started him in Sunday school, but up until now I have had to stay in the classroom with him.

Will he learn to be more independent as he grows older?

What would you advise me to do?

Since I do not know you or the child, I cannot give you a pat answer. There are so many variables in child development and so many variables in the interaction of personalities within a home—and outside the home.

However, I would advise you to be alert to the possibility of being an overly protective mother. The tendency to overprotection usually springs from the mother's sense of anxiety, and she may transfer this feeling of anxiety to her child. A mother who becomes aware of an overprotective attitude should resist the impulse to rescue her child whenever he gets involved in activities that appear to be a bit dangerous, like climbing up on chairs or crawling into cupboards. He can usually solve these problems if left to himself. The behavior of a mother who anxiously rushes to a child's rescue convinces him that there are dangers all around and that he needs the constant attention of his mother if he is to survive.

I think you will experience less trouble when you take your child to his Sunday school room if you follow these suggestions: Take your son where other children play—daily, if possible—at a nearby playground, for instance. Invite neighbor children to play in your yard—or in your home, if the weather is inclement. When he plays with other children, then he can learn that children are noisy and rough—and often mean—compared with the adults he knows. He can learn that despite these characteristics in children they are fun to be with. Give your child a reasonable opportunity to learn how to defend himself in minor squabbles. I say this because you may find yourself watching your child constantly when he plays with other children and spring to his protection if it seems that another child is going to hurt him.

I take it that this child is your firstborn, so I pass on to you this information gleaned by pediatricians from parents with several children: The first child has always had more trouble getting acquainted with outsiders and learning to enjoy rough-and-tumble play; he is timid in the face of new situations; he has always clung to the parents and demanded a lot of attention from them.

I would advise you to make use of baby-sitters on a fairly regular basis so that your child will learn that there are times when you will go away without him and will return. Don't sneak away from him. Let him know you are going away, even though it means that he will cry for a while. When he sees that his crying doesn't get him what he wants, he will stop crying.

I am quite sure that as you give your child opportunities for give-and-take with other children he will become more independent. Children learn much from other children.

Dear Frances,

My problem is my six-year-old son. I also have a four-year-old and a baby one year old. They keep me busy, but I love them dearly.

My eldest has become a real problem. He resists going to school, both in the morning and at noon. Let me explain. He has gone to a Bible pre-kindergarten. That was when he was four and a half. He did wonderfully well, even though he had to get up earlier than he does now. Last year he went to kindergarten. Since the session was from 10:30 to 12:45, the time when he left for school created a problem because he would be absorbed in playing and then would have to leave his play. We really had some battles then.

This year I thought things were better, but I guess I was wrong. He seems to enjoy school after he gets there, and brings home his papers for us to see. My husband and I have talked nicely to him, we have scolded, and even yelled at him—to no avail. He still resists going to school. Both my husband and I have had college education, and we realize how important these early years are for our son.

I pray for this child every day. I admit that sometimes I yell when I shouldn't. I have prayed about this also and am trying very hard not to yell. . . . I want to do what God wants me to do.

I do pray that you can give me the help I need. I need help from someone outside our family.

27

I can understand why your child would feel frustrated about leaving his play when he had to go to kindergarten at 10:30 in the morning. It's natural for a child to hate to leave his play. But when your child makes a fuss about doing something that will have to be a regular part of his daily routine, all you can do is to maintain a firm attitude as you see to it that your child gets off to school.

It would be easy to tell you not to get angry when dealing with this child. However, since anger is your natural reaction to a frustrating situation, I would urge you to ask God to enable you to control your anger and to act in a calm manner.

It seems to me that your child's problem is not one of not liking school but of not wanting to break away from home to go to school. It may be that he is too attached to you. A friend of mine had an adopted daughter who feared to go to school because she feared leaving her mother; she was afraid Mother wouldn't be there when she returned from school.

In my reading on the subject of children's fears, I learned that around age four a child may develop a sudden fear of animals, of being hurt, of death, and of having his parents leave him, even to go out to dinner. Around five or six, his major fear is that his mother won't come home.

Parents of a fearful child are bound to ask; "Does a child ever get over such fears?" With careful handling, all his fears will be on the way out by the time he is eight. By age nine, they will be gone.

Dr. T. R. Van Dellen, in his newspaper feature, "How to Keep Your Child Well," discussed a child's fear of going to school, under the title, "School Phobia." He said;

> The school phobia often is masked by legitimate-sounding complaints—tummy ache, nausea, or headache. If the tot is permitted to stay home, he gives himself away

by getting well a half hour later. The causes for this type of fear are many. It may stem from alarm at leaving home. But often the basic fault lies with Mother. She may be poorly adjusted to marriage and has invested all her love in the child, usually an only child.

In other instances, something has happened at school or among the playmates. The personality and development of the boy or girl may be responsible for the school phobia, but more often the personality and attitudes of the parents are to blame.[1]

From a *Parents' Magazine* article titled "The Big, Bad Fears of Childhood," I discovered that parents' reactions to a child's fears at school age, as at all ages, are most important. The authors, John E. Allen, M.D. and Frances H. Allen, advised parents to treat children of that age who have fears as they would treat them at an earlier age.

The treatment referred to involves "great parental patience" and avoidance of "bulldozing methods to cure a child of his temperamental outbursts—that only prolongs the outbursts and intensifies the crises." Parents were advised to "talk out and explain the fears, within reason," and to remember that "though ridiculing or ignoring fears is unhealthy, oversolicitude about them is also unwise. Coddling has a tendency to make a child fear new situations, new places, and new people."

This example was given:

> The mother who repeatedly drives her son one block to a playmate's house because he is afraid of getting lost, or who regularly sits outside the Sunday-school classroom to lend emotional support to her offspring within does not help her child overcome his fears and grow toward independence.

---

1. *Chicago Sunday Tribune,* March 16, 1960. Used by permission of the author.

I share with you the authors' suggestions about how to treat the fears of a child when starting school:

> Because he's now also responding to school pressures, don't set goals that are too difficult for him. This will only add to his tensions and anxieties and may lead him back into babyish ways, such as having temper tantrums or bed-wetting episodes. If such episodes should occur, don't worry. They are signs to you to ease up a bit and wait patiently. This kind of "regressive" behavior, if not made too much of, is usually quite temporary.
>
> Wise parents can help their children put fear in its proper place. Susie, for example, feared and hated school. Talking to her, her mother discovered the fear was caused by the simple problem of getting on and off the school bus. Susie was afraid of dropping her lunch box or her books and being laughed at by the more experienced passengers. Her mother was wise enough not to ridicule this fear. Instead, she walked to the bus with her and when it arrived, said, "Be sure to get off at the right stop."
>
> "You're silly," said the child, laughing. "That's school, of course!"
>
> And Susie forgot the problem of her lunch box and books.[2]

In *Child Psychology* by Arthur T. Jersild, I found these helpful paragraphs on the subject of sending children off to school:

> For many children, the beginning of their school career in the first grade or kindergarten marks a radical departure from their previous way of life. The youngster is now legally and psychologically in the custody of someone outside the home several hours of the day. All children are probably deeply impressed with the important step they are taking. Some children move eagerly into this new phase of existence; some have looked forward to school for a long time; but for many children it is a time of stress.

2. March 1964, p. 150. Used by permission of the publisher.

Quite a few show the strain openly through an increase in "behavior problems," or by clinging to their parents, crying, or making a scene during the first day or even during the first few weeks of school. We cannot, however, judge a child's feelings, whether of joy or of distress, at this juncture of his life simply by noting his smiles or his tears.

In one investigation in which the same children were studied as they moved from kindergarten into the elementary-school grades, the children who were most explosive in showing their feelings about entering school made as good an adjustment and, if anything, a better adjustment to school in the long run than those who seemed to take the venture calmly. This finding may have other meanings, but it suggests that children who seem distressed when entering school may be no more deeply stirred than those who remain outwardly calm; the difference may be that some youngsters freely express their emotions while others keep them hidden. . . . It is quite common for children to feel deeply moved when they enter a new phase in their careers. And it is not the children alone who are moved, for many parents also feel a surge of emotion. When a child sets off for school, his departure is a symbol of a larger undertaking. The child is taking an important step on a long road; at the end of the road, if all goes well, he will no longer be a child but an independent adult. It is no wonder, therefore, that many parents, while pleased that their child is growing up, also feel a tightening at the throat as they watch him leave home for his first day at school.[3]

So I would advise you to try to understand what your child is going through and to try to understand your own attitudes. Curb your desire to yell at your child. Relax, and endeavor to be patient while you wait for the development that will bring about a change in your child's attitude toward leaving home to go to school.

---

3. Fifth ed. (Englewood Cliffs, N.J.: Prentice-Hall, 1960), pp. 200-201. By permission of Prentice-Hall, Inc., Englewood Cliffs, N.J.

As a Christian parent, you can depend on God to strengthen you to be patient. See Colossians 1:11.

Dear Frances,

After hearing you speak on the subject of "Teaching Your Children the Value of Money," I purchased for my ten-year-old girl and eleven-year-old boy a cash journal in which they record how they spend their allowance. Both are receiving an allowance of one dollar a week.

My question is this: Should I deduct, as a punishment, a certain amount from their allowance if they fail to carry out duties I have assigned them?

My advice is this: Do not deduct anything from their allowance when they fail to care for certain duties. When you deduct amounts from their allowance for this reason, then it appears that the allowance is *pay* for duties performed. Furthermore, you're apt to get into haggling situations.

In my opinion, chores suited to a child's ability should be performed by him without thought of remuneration. Because children are members of a family, they share in the privileges of a home. They should likewise share to some extent in the responsibilities.

Keep in mind that an allowance should be considered a tool for teaching a child how to handle money, not payment for chores.

Dear Frances,

Is it natural for a child of eleven and a half (a boy) to rebel and seem indifferent to the Christian ways of our family? We attend church services twice on Sunday and Sunday school, also prayer meeting and Bible classes during the week. This boy learns his lessons, and yet his attitude seems to be one of indifference. We have Bible reading and prayer at mealtimes but cannot get him to establish a habit of reading the Bible for himself.

I am quite concerned about him and spend much time in praying for him. I also pray with him.

Parents cannot expect that because they are faithful in attending church, Sunday school, prayer meeting, and Bible classes their children will automatically enjoy such activities. As godly T. J. Bach used to say, "God has no grandchildren." Our children are not children of God just because we are. They too must personally receive Jesus as their Saviour. For some children this experience comes early in life, while for others it comes later.

I hope that what I'm going to say next doesn't appear to be a criticism of your church. Many times the young people feel that the sermons they hear and the teaching they get in Sunday school are not relevant. What they hear isn't geared to their personal needs. Of course, as a young person matures, he will not look upon the ministry of the Word of God from the pulpit and in the classroom only in the light of his particular needs but also in the light of the needs of others. God has many children in His family, and their needs are varied. A sermon preached one Sunday may not meet a particular young person's most pressing needs, but in all likelihood it is meeting the needs of other individuals.

You can be thankful that your boy learns his lessons. He is being indoctrinated with biblical truth. The seed of the Word of God is being planted in his mind and heart. And God has promised that His word shall not return unto Him void, or empty of results (Isaiah 55:11).

You say that your boy seems indifferent. However, you cannot always tell by appearances what a young person's true attitude is. As a boy enters adolescence, he tends to withdraw into himself. He is less open with his parents.

Often what his peers think of him matters more to him than what his parents think of him.

Another characteristic of the adolescent is his tendency to rebel. He wants to assert himself as an individual. This is part of his growing-up process.

If we believe what the Bible teaches, another point to consider is this: All of us are born with a sinful nature. All of us have an inborn tendency—a natural bent—to rebel against authority. This propensity is described thus in Isaiah 53:6: "All we like sheep have gone astray; we have turned every one to his own way." All of us—adults as well as adolescents—are making choices every day, choices that involve saying either yes or no to what we know is right and good.

I'm wondering if your son has definitely received Jesus as his Saviour, if he is born again and thus a child of God. If he isn't a child of God, then it is natural that he will not enjoy reading the Bible for himself.

On the other hand, he may be a Christian who lacks interest in reading the Bible because he finds it difficult to understand the King James Version of the Bible. He may find it easier to read the Bible with understanding and enjoyment if you place in his hands a version in contemporary language. You might want to give him a copy of paraphrase like *The Living Bible*. The language is such that young people can easily grasp the meaning of passages which seem ambiguous to them as they read the King James Version (translated more than 350 years ago).

Spiritual growth cannot be forced. It must come from within. If you have done your best in bringing your son up in the knowledge of the Bible with the benefit of family Bible reading and prayer and regular participation in church activities, then your chief responsibility in the adolescent years is to love him and pray for him. As you wait for his commitment to Christ and for the spiritual growth you want to see, remind yourself of this: When you plant a seed, it takes time for it to germinate and grow into a plant. You can give a plant good soil, proper temperature and moisture, but after that you must stand back and wait for the growth that must come from the life within.

I would counsel you to let your son know that you expect him to attend the services of your church and Sunday school along with the rest of your family. However, I would advise you to avoid putting pressure on him in the area of personal devotions. Faithfulness in personal Bible reading and prayer must spring out of a sincere love for the Lord and a desire for fellowship with Him.

Expect God to use His Word in your son's life. Expect God to answer your prayers for your boy. Also pray for his Sunday school teacher, for the youth workers of your church and your minister, that God will guide them and enable them to make the truths of the Bible relevant to the needs of your son and others like him. Also pray for yourself, asking that your life may show the reality of your love for him and for the Lord.

And Those Teenagers

Dear Frances,

My daughter Sharon is a freshman in high school, and I've been having problems with her. She's a quiet girl, is very good-looking, and neat in her appearance. Her personality isn't what it should be, and as a result, she doesn't make and keep friends. She is a loner. She professes to be a Christian but evidently doesn't fully realize what is involved in being a Christian.

She has been reared in the church, with certain rules and regulations to follow. I might say that we are members of a liberal church where most of the people seem to be unconcerned about whom their children date. Since my husband usually works on Sunday, our children and I have been going to another church where we are satisfied with what is preached. But their coldness is intolerable. The women aren't friendly to me, and the girls aren't at all friendly to Sharon.

The boys go for her, and she is constantly involved in a companionship with some boy. So far I haven't allowed her to date, as we have set the age at which she may begin dating at sixteen.

In order to keep her from sneaking, I have permitted her to receive phone calls, and boys are allowed to come to our house. Her present interest is a nineteen-year-old boy. We haven't permitted her to go out with him in the evening. The closeness of the relationship between them has been kept a secret from me until this past weekend. She is now begging for permission to go out with him in the evening. I have denied her request. She spends her free time at school with him, and I have no control over this. My husband and I would like to break off the relationship, as we feel this young man is too experienced for our daughter.

To complicate matters, my husband and I are divided about the question of which church we should attend. He refuses to discuss this subject. He also refuses to desist from browbeating our daughter. He is a strong, rigid disciplinarian and is disgusted with both Sharon and me. He says the blame lies entirely on me. He doesn't have to remind me that I've failed. I'm fully aware of this. He is constantly telling me that Sharon and I are stupid. He tells her this all the time. I think this is wrong.

We have discovered that Sharon is now smoking. He told her that she is lost because of this. I told her that I didn't believe this. I let her know that I was disappointed and asked her to try to quit smoking. I hope she will be able to abstain.

Sharon is almost an exact copy of me when I was her age, with this exception: I was better grounded in my faith. Emotionally, I was very insecure and longed desperately to acquire friends.

I realize this kind of problem is common. The question is, How can Sharon's personality be improved? I think, if she were humble and friendly, she would have more appeal to other girls. I too need to develop a better personality. For one thing, I am too outspoken!

How do others handle a situation like ours? The tighter I pull the reins, the more Sharon rebels and sneaks.

It seems to me that your daughter is a classic example of a teenage girl who is starved for love and approval. Many girls who turn to older men do so because they haven't received love and affection from their fathers. Your husband certainly is making a mistake when he calls Sharon stupid. If he has been doing this for many years, she probably believes what he says and for that reason is withdrawn and has become a loner, to use your description.

Your husband is also wrong in telling her she is lost because she smokes. People are lost because they do not believe on the Lord Jesus Christ as the One who died for their sins on the cross of Calvary. No one is excluded from God's family, nor is eternal salvation withheld, because an individual smokes.

Since your husband is a rigid disciplinarian, he may have failed to express love to Sharon through the early years of her childhood development. During the early teens many a girl and her mother go through what is called "mother-daughter antagonism." A girl can keep on a fairly even keel, even when she is at swords' points with her mother, if she is sure of the love, understanding, and approval of her father. A girl's father, if she loves him and looks up to him, gives her a pattern of the kind of a man she will look for in the man she will marry.

I think a great deal of damage has already been done to Sharon through lack of unity between you and your husband. Often parents who are one in their aims and goals find the years when their children are in their teens very difficult, but when a husband and wife consistently fail to show unity, discipline of their children becomes much more difficult.

Criticism of your church doesn't help either. When parents are critical of their church, it becomes easy for children to question the authority of the church.

One more point: It seems to me that you don't accept

yourself. Because of your mentioning that you're not satisfied with your personality and your reference to your lack
of emotional security as a girl and your desperate longing
to acquire friends, I am wondering if this is why you do
not accept Sharon's personality. Why try to change her
personality? Allow her to be herself. After all, by the time
our children enter high school their personality patterns
are pretty well set. They have by then passed the years
when they were more impressionable and more easily
molded.

You are concerned about Sharon's personality, about
her relationships with the nineteen-year-old boy, about her
smoking and her insecurity, but you haven't expressed any
concern about her need for love and her need to know
Jesus in a vital personal relationship—as Saviour, Lord,
and loyal Friend. Even if she doesn't have many friends
among her peers, even if you and her father are not in
agreement about what church to attend and how to guide
her, even if she doesn't receive from her parents the love
she needs, she can find a wonderful love and companionship through knowing Jesus as Saviour and Lord. It's possible for her to experience what is expressed in a contemporary gospel song: "I found what I wanted when I found
the Lord."

If I were you, I would earnestly pray that she might
enter into a vital relationship with the Lord. Also, I would
confess to her how you have failed her, talk with her about
how you felt when you were a girl, tell her you love her,
and show love to her in every way you can. But loving
her and showing love doesn't mean that you will need to
pamper her. Hold to your decision that she is not to date
until she is sixteen. When she starts dating, restrict dating
nights to Friday and Saturday during the school year. Also
set a time when she must be home.

I don't know what advice to give about trying to break

up her friendship with the young man. Usually the more parents try to break up such a friendship the more determined a girl like Sharon will be to continue the friendship. I would talk with her about how you feel about the difference in their ages—that while a four-year age difference will not seem so great when a girl marries in her twenties or thirties, she still has three more years of high school before her. She will have more fun during those years if she dates boys of high school age. Present the wisdom of developing many friendships instead of going steady with one person. Going steady often leads to a teenage marriage—sometimes to a person the girl would not choose if she waited until she was in her twenties to get married.

As you talk with her, give her opportunity to talk. School yourself to listen to her. Keep your emotions under control.

One more thing you can do is this: You can wage a battle for her spiritual welfare through intercessory prayer. The Bible tells us, in James 5:16, that the fervent prayer of a righteous man is effective in its working. Pray for yourself and your husband, too, that you may become better persons and—perhaps—be able to regain some of the ground you have lost in your relationships with your daughter.

Dear Frances,

I am writing to you in the hope that you will be able to give me a little advice and encouragement.

We adopted two girls (one at a time in infancy). We gave them a Christian training, but I must confess I am heartbroken over how my eldest daughter has turned out. She has lived immorally and is now married to a non-Christian man. She isn't happy with him. She has thrown our Christian teachings overboard and resents all my pleas for her to repent and live for Jesus Christ.

41

Now my youngest daughter (only eighteen) is talking about getting married in a few months. She has gone with the boy (also eighteen) for over a year. I tried to discourage her going steady with him—but to no avail. She now is engaged and has a diamond, against my wishes. He is going to a mechanics school and will complete that training in ten months. He seems like a fairly good boy. He goes to church with my daughter, but I don't think he is a real Christian. (He doesn't know enough about what is involved in being a Christian.)

I feel my daughter is immature and that she would later regret getting married.

They know I am opposed to their getting married at such an early age. They are beginning to look at me as an "enemy" because I'm not in favor of their getting married. The boy's folks are for the marriage and will sign for their son (that is, give their consent).

What would you do if you were in my place? Should I try to get them to see a "family counselor," or should I go along with their desire to get married, and give them my blessing? I want to do what's right and yet be friends with my children.

I will surely appreciate any advice you give me.

I'm sorry for the way things have turned out in your older daughter's experience. I hope you don't attribute her conduct to the fact that she is adopted, for children to whom parents give birth bring similar heartaches to their parents. Even though parents are faithful in giving their children Christian training, yet they have the power of choice, which they can use to follow God's will or to follow the way of self-indulgence and self-will. I would advise you to refrain from nagging her about the wrong decisions she has made. If she is a believer in Jesus Christ, she is all too conscious of her wrongdoing, and God by His Holy Spirit will be speaking to her conscience and calling her to repent and live for Him. God loves her more than you do. The reason she resents your pleas is that she already knows what she should do, and doesn't have to be reminded again and again. Keep loving her and praying for her.

Regarding your youngest daughter, I would counsel you to cease expressing your opposition to her marriage. Usually, when parents openly and persistently show their opposition to the plans of a couple to marry, the young people become more determined than ever to marry. Human nature is obstinate. When something is forbidden, that is what we want. Wanting the forbidden began in the Garden of Eden with Adam and Eve and has continued ever since.

I think that once you have thoroughly talked over the advantages you see in waiting to get married and have set before your daughter God's standard (that believers should not be unequally yoked with unbelievers), you should drop the subject as far as conversation about it is concerned. But continue to pray for both of them.

As young adults, *they* are responsible for their choices— not *you*.

If you continue to oppose the marriage, they will get married anyhow and may break off all communication with you. Instead, look upon this young man as a person who can be won to the Lord.

We older people need to remind ourselves that our young people are in what is called the "now" generation. They want to enjoy life *now,* for they are uncertain of what the future holds in this period that is unprecedented in the number of changes taking place and in the rapidity of changes. If a young man and a young woman are in love and want to enjoy that love in the bonds of marriage, as God has ordained, I think it is better not to stand in

43

their way if you see that they are fully determined to get married.

Dear Frances,

My twenty-year-old son is now a member of a cult that holds a false view of biblical truth. This boy was a professing Christian before he accepted the teachings of this cult through the influence of a girl with whom he was going.

I've prayed and prayed, and I have talked and talked to him. I've bought books that point out the error in this system of teaching, only to see him become more and more involved.

I am very discouraged, very much afraid he will influence his younger brother (eighteen years old). I get the feeling that God is punishing us for having failed to faithfully teach our children His Word. . . . God seems so far away from me, and I wonder whether I ever was a Christian. Am I just a pretender? I honestly want to be a Christian mother, but sometimes I wonder.

I know the Bible says, "Rejoice in the Lord alway" and "in everything give thanks," but I just can't seem to do this. In spite of prayers—many prayers—of friends and relatives, this dear son steadfastly goes the other way.

Maybe I'm sick in mind. I just keep thinking about his acceptance of this false teaching day and night, and how terrible it is; also how I've failed my family and God. I think like this day in and day out, and I know such thinking doesn't glorify God at all. But I feel helpless. It seems like God has forsaken me. . . .

Can you help me get straightened out? What is wrong that I seem so powerless? How do you deal with a follower of a false cult who lives right in your home? What can I do to keep my younger son from becoming involved?

My heart ached for you as I read your letter telling about your concern for both your sons. You have been bearing a heavy burden.

God wants us to be concerned about the spiritual welfare of those we love. However, we must remember that we cannot make decisions for our children. Each person must make his own decisions, and each is responsible for the results of his choices.

Regarding the responsibility of parents for their children, we who are parents can aim to create in our home, by the kind of persons we are, an atmosphere that will prepare our children for a positive response to God's love and His invitation to salvation. Parents, by *direct* teaching about God and by *indirect* teaching (by the kind of persons they are and how they live) have a good deal of influence on their children. But only God can give the illumination that gives the spiritual light needed before conversion. When such a light is given and our loved ones see clearly what God offers and their need of what He offers, they can say yes or no to God, just as we (their parents) can say yes or no to God. We can say yes or no to God just as Adam and Eve, our first parents, could. They could have chosen to say yes to God by obeying Him in the garden of Eden. Instead, they said no to God when they chose to yield to Satan's temptation.

By the time your children reach high school age the major part of your teaching responsibility in your home has been completed. The most impressionable years are past. Soon your children will be adults and making their own decisions. You cannot force them to believe in Jesus Christ. They must decide what they will do with Jesus, the Son of God sent to be the Saviour of the world.

I realize that you feel guilty because you haven't given your children a better grounding in the essential truths of the Bible. You are quite sure that if you had been more faithful your eldest son would not have succumbed to the teaching of the cult to which you referred. I would say that most parents feel they have failed in one aspect or another of their parental responsibility, or at least they feel they should have done a better job than they have. In many homes parents tell their children by their actions that they consider other things more important than the Word of God. What are we teaching our children when we fail to teach them from the Bible what they need to know in order to become God's children and to live victoriously as Christians, or when we fail to attend Sunday school and church services?

But what is past is past. What can you do now?

You can pray *for* your children (on their behalf), and you can pray *against* the power of Satan in their lives, asking God to restrain and hinder the power of Satan in their lives. Satan has the power to blind men's minds lest they see the light of the gospel and believe (2 Corinthians 4:4). Satan is referred to in the Bible as a deceiver, and he uses his power to deceive by making sin appear glamorous, and by making false teaching appear to be the truth.

A Christian parent can claim the victory that Jesus Christ gained over Satan on the cross of Calvary. (See Colossians 2:14-15, where we read that Jesus triumphed over principalities and powers when He died on the cross.)

The power of prayer is graphically depicted in the twelfth chapter of Acts, where we read about the apostle Peter being held in prison. The circumstances were not at all favorable, for Herod planned to execute Peter. However, we read this in verse 5 of that chapter: *"But* prayer was made without ceasing of the church unto God for him."* As a result, the chains fell off Peter's hands, and he was led out of the prison by an angel.

Even though Christian parents recognize the power of prayer and make use of the weapon of prayer, they also

46

need to recognize that a law of sowing and reaping is operating in human lives. We read about this law in the Bible: "Whatsoever a man soweth, that shall he also reap" (Galatians 6:7). If parents have been careless about teaching their children and have neglected giving them a sound foundation in biblical truths; if they have been careless in personal relationships in their home, failing to show love; and if they have been careless about living righteously, they are going to reap what they have sown—not only in their lives but in their children's lives.

If you have failed in the ways I have mentioned, all you can do now is: confess your failures and ask God to forgive you. You can also ask God to show mercy in saving your children. Then try to forget what is past and concentrate now—*today*—on being the kind of person God wants you to be. Keep feeding your inner man on the Word of God, for this will strengthen your faith in God. Keep setting your mind on "those things which are above" (Colossians 3:1). This would include thinking much about God's love (for you and those you love), His faithfulness to His promises, His power, His ability to so arrange the circumstances of the lives of your loved ones that they will recognize their need of Him. Remember, God loves them more than you do. So commit them to Him.

I would also suggest that you talk less about the matters on which you do not agree. They may feel you are nagging. Talk less to them, but talk more to God—about them.

Refuse to go round and round in the groove of fretting and fearfulness. The more you go round and round in the same groove, the deeper it becomes. You must by an effort of your will turn your thinking to other channels, just as you turn the knob on your radio or TV set to change programs.

I repeat, *forget* what is past, as Paul the apostle said

he did, and press on in the path that lies before you, living life today as God would have you live it.

Ask God to lead you on to maturity. Maturity involves growth in discernment and in love, which will mean that you will abound more and more in love toward your family members, with the kind of love that frees them instead of binding them to you, recognizing that they are responsible for their own decisions.

About an Errant Husband

Dear Frances,

I would appreciate so much any comments you might make concerning the situation here in my home, in direct relationship to my husband.

I want to say, first of all, that John is a wonderful husband and father, and he and I have had eighteen years of happy marriage. When I was saved, I prayed that he too would believe in Jesus Christ and that we might serve Him together. John has attended church with me ever since I began living for the Lord, and he has gradually become involved in activities such as class parties, driving the church bus, serving on committees, working on our new sanctuary, and is now serving as missionary treasurer. I thank God that he enjoys doing all these things. He enjoys the fellowship of Christians and attends the annual retreat for men of our church. Together we went to a couples' retreat some months ago. So what more could I ask for?

Well, the problem is this: I really do not feel that John has been born again. Not once have I seen him read God's Word or pray, nor have I observed that he feels at ease talking about the Lord on a spiritual basis. He talks about the church and is a good listener in a conversation about spiritual things but resents being "pinned down," so to speak, about his own needs. I haven't done this in many years, but I am very concerned about him. Since he is a quiet person and is difficult to communicate with at times, I pray about the matter of his relationship to the Lord and try to leave it with the Lord. I'm sure that there are those who know us who would be surprised that I have these doubts about John's salvation, and they would perhaps feel I am judging. I hope I'm not doing this.

Last spring we had evangelistic meetings at our church, which is a very fundamental, soul-winning church. The evangelist told me he felt my husband was a very troubled man. This same evangelist told me he had been similarly impressed about my husband during a previous series of meetings at our church.

After my conversation with the evangelist, I realized that John did not raise his hand at a meeting where an invitation was given for those who knew they were going to heaven to raise their hands. Up to that time I had tried to convince myself that he was a Christian. Sometimes he will seem to be under deep conviction during a message, and at other times he seems completely unmoved when others are deeply moved by the Spirit of God.

Perhaps you know of someone who has had a similar experience and could offer me some advice on what to do about it. I have hesitated to speak openly of this matter for fear my husband may become bitter and turn away from associations with Christian people and the activities of the church. On the other hand, my speaking to him about this matter might encourage him to make a definite decision to receive Jesus Christ as Saviour.

Any comments?

I can see why you are concerned about your husband's relationship to the Lord, for it is possible for a person to associate with Christians, to attend church services regularly, enjoy the social get-togethers of Christian couples, and serve in various capacities within the church organization without being a Christian. We do not become Christians by osmosis, by close association with those who are Christians. We do not become Christians by engaging in good works, in church-related activities. We are not born Christians because we are born of Christian parents. Godly T. J. Bach used to say, "God has no grandchildren."

We are born into God's family one by one, by a spiritual birth. The Word of God teaches that this birth follows the definite act of receiving Jesus Christ as Saviour. We read in the Gospel of John: "As many as received him, to them gave he power [or, the right] to become the sons of God, even to them that believe on his name: which were born, not of blood, nor of the will of the flesh, nor of the will of man, but of God" (1:12-13).

It is recorded in the third chapter of John that Jesus told Nicodemus, a ruler of the Jews (a religious man with high ethical standards), "Except a man be born again, he cannot see the kingdom of God. . . . That which is born of the flesh is flesh; and that which is born of the Spirit is spirit."

Men and women must be born of the Spirit of God if they are to be children of God and enter the Kingdom of God. All their high moral standards, all their good works, all their philanthropy and church activity will avail nothing in establishing a relationship with God whereby they will become children of God. God forgives our sins and justifies us (declares us righteous) because we believe on Jesus as our Saviour, the One who died for our sins on the cross of Calvary. God sends His Holy Spirit to live in those who thus believe in Jesus Christ. This is what is involved in the new birth, the beginning of a new life as a child of God. After an individual experiences the impartation of this new life from God, then he can begin

51

to grow in the grace and knowledge of the Lord Jesus Christ and go on to spiritual maturity.

I am sure, from what you have told me, that your husband has enough knowledge to make an intelligent decision to receive Jesus Christ as Saviour. This is what we might call illumination. But after light is given, individuals must choose whether to accept or reject it.

It seems to be the business of Satan to hinder illumination of the mind, for we read in 2 Corinthians 4:4 that "the god of this world [Satan] hath blinded the minds of them which believe not, lest the light of the glorious gospel of Christ, who is the image of God, should shine unto them."

Not only does Satan seek to hinder illumination of the mind by blinding their minds but he also seeks to hinder that act of the will which decides for Christ by deceiving men, persuading them that the truth is a lie or that it isn't necessary to make a decision right now, for there will be plenty of time for that later. I think Satan hinders some people from making a decision for Christ because he persuades them that the demands of Christ on His followers are too rigorous and will require too much self-denial.

Once a decision for Jesus Christ has been made by an individual, Satan continues to oppose the work of God's Spirit. This is indicated by this admonition written by the apostle Peter: "Be sober, be vigilant; because your *adversary* the devil, as a roaring lion, walketh about, seeking whom he may devour" (1 Peter 5:8).

Since Satan is the spiritual adversary of both Christians and non-Christians, it is no wonder that the apostle Paul wrote to the Christians at Ephesus: "We wrestle not against flesh and blood, but against principalities, against powers, against the rulers of the darkness of this world, against spiritual wickedness in high places" (Ephesians 6:12). This is the reason the apostle Paul told those

Christians to take unto them the spiritual armor described in Ephesians 6:13-17. After they took unto them this armor that would enable them to stand against Satan's attacks, they were to pray always with "all prayer and supplication in the Spirit."

As we think of praying for individuals, there are two ways we can pray: (1) *against* the power of Satan, asking God to overrule, to hold back, to hinder the power of Satan, and (2) *for* the person about whom we are concerned, that he may experience victory.

In my opinion, prayer is your greatest resource. Pray for your husband, and pray against the power of Satan in his life.

Be sensitive to the leading of the Spirit of God about when and how to speak to your husband about the absolute necessity of making a definite, personal decision to receive Jesus Christ as Saviour. Be sure that you speak to him out of a heart of love and in such a way that he senses you are not critical of him but concerned for him. Ask God to guide you in communicating with your husband so that he may not resent what you say. Believe that God will prepare his heart, as He prepared the heart of Lydia, the first convert of Paul's ministry in Europe. It is recorded in Acts 16:14 that the Lord opened her heart so "that she attended unto the things which were spoken of Paul."

Once you have spoken clearly and definitely about your concern for your husband's spiritual welfare, let the matter rest and wait for the Spirit of God to work in your husband's mind and heart. And do not attempt to judge whether he is under conviction or not by outward appearances. We learn from 1 Samuel 16:7 that "the Lord seeth not as a man seeth; for man looketh on the outward appearance, but the Lord looketh on the heart."

Do emphasize, as you talk with your husband, the importance of his will. He must make the choice. God will not do this for him.

Dear Frances,

During the early part of my marriage I caught my husband lying to me about small things. As a result I have lost confidence in him and find myself criticizing him all the time. Please help me, or suggest some way for my husband to break this habit.

It's clear from the teaching of the Bible that lying is sin. In Colossians 3:9-10 we find what the apostle Paul told first century Christians: "Lie not to one another, seeing that ye have put off the old man with his deeds; and have put on the new man, which is renewed in knowledge after the image of him that created him." He also wrote in another epistle: "Wherefore putting away lying, speak every man truth with his neighbor: for we are members one of another" (Ephesians 4:25). In the list of evil things that Jesus said proceed from within a man—from his heart, we find that "false witness" is one of the evil things that defile a man (Matthew 15:19).

It's easy, if your besetting sin isn't lying, to condemn and criticize the person whose besetting sin is lying. But criticizing the person won't help him. Telling him it is sin and expecting him to ask your forgiveness and God's won't help him to overcome this habit.

It may help you to realize how complex your husband's problem may be if we consider the causes of lying in children, remembering that this grown person who habitually lies is immature, that is, like a child.

When children lie, we recognize that exaggerating— telling big stories—is a part of their immaturity. The child who exaggerates needs to be corrected and helped without labeling him a liar. Labeling doesn't help. But you should aim to help him distinguish between a make-believe story and a true story. And you can teach him that God expects us to tell the truth to one another, and you can point out that Jesus (as a boy and as a man) always told the truth.

A common form of lying is the defensive lie. When a child is faced with the possibility of punishment or correction, he may lie in order to avoid the consequences of his actions. In marriage, a husband may lie to his wife because he can't bear to face up to what she will think or what she will say to him if she knows the truth about him—his failures, for instance.

Children who have serious feelings of inferiority may create false stories in order to gain the approval of others. Feeling unworthy and rejected by others, this kind of person thinks he can impress others if he tells stories which "build him up." In other words, he is playacting.

A person who is insecure and jealous may create a lie about another person to express feelings of hostility and resentment. The jealous person may really want to attack this other person, but, being too fearful, he starts a rumor about his enemy. This is his attempt to get revenge.

A person who continually lies and practices deceit may be suffering from a serious personality disturbance. The delinquent or anti-social person is often found to have a consistent pattern of deceit. For instance, a teenage boy who steals and drinks must cover his actions with false accounts of his activities if he is to avoid punishment he fears.

If a person has never been converted, you should not be surprised that he lies, for, as we read in the writings of the prophet Jeremiah, "The heart is deceitful above all things, and desperately wicked: who can know it?" (Jeremiah 17:9).

Even a Christian may have difficulty with lying. Unless we are continually controlled by the Holy Spirit, it is possible for any of us to yield to the impulses of our

55

fleshly nature. And one of these is the impulse to lie. Lying is a work of the flesh.

In dealing with anyone, child or immature adult, who is troubled with lying, you should avoid a judgmental attitude. Instead, you ought to view him with compassion, for this person's lying is a symptom of something deeper. He may be a person who feels inferior and uses lying to prove his adequacy to others, to bolster his ego.

Let this person know you love him, just as he is. Let him know that God loves him, that he is significant to God, that God has a purpose for each person He has created and that this purpose can be fulfilled as we put our lives into His hands. God so loved this person that He gave His Son to die for him. If he believes on God's Son, God will forgive his sins—all of his sins. If he comes to see that he is precious to God, a person of worth, a person beloved but one in whom some changes need to be made, then he can rely on God to make him into the kind of person God wants him to be.

Dr. Clyde Narramore, Christian psychologist and counselor, says, "The person who lies will not likely change his behaviour unless he comes to a clear understanding of the causes of his problem. . . . This person must see that lying doesn't just happen. There is a reason—and it can be found. Once it is found, it can be overcome."[1]

This statement would seem to indicate that professional counseling is needed by your husband. Of course, a man may be insulted by his wife's suggestion that he seek such counseling, and refuse to make an appointment with a counselor. If this should be the reaction of your husband, then I would suggest that you ask God to enable you to love your husband with a love that is greater than the kind of love which is our response to a person's admirable

---

1. *Counseling with Youth at Church, School, and Camp* (Grand Rapids: Zondervan, 1966), p. 84.

qualities. This kind of love is the fruit of the Holy Spirit (Galatians 5:22). Say aloud every day, as you think of him, "God loves him, and I love him, too."

Avoid an attitude of moral superiority. Also, beware of being perfectionist in your attitude. If your husband loves you very much, your perfectionism may prompt him to lie, for he cannot bear not to have your approval.

Just as God loves us even though He cannot always approve of our conduct, so we ought to love those of whose conduct we cannot approve.

Dear Frances,

I'm in desperate need of help and counseling.

I'm thirty-four years old, trained as a nurse, although I'm not working now. I have been married for twelve years to a school teacher, and we have three lovely daughters (ages eleven, ten, and four).

About six weeks ago my husband, whom I love very much, announced to me during an argument that he didn't love me anymore. He also told me he hadn't loved me for at least six years. Needless to say, I was horrified, shocked, and hurt. Everything seemed to crumble under my feet.

Yes, we have had disagreements through the years. Yes, I have failed him in many ways. But I always felt that our love was strong enough to last through all these differences.

We talked many hours. I asked his forgiveness. I asked him how I had failed him. He responded that he not only didn't love me but had no desire to regain that love. Since then we have prayed to God to help restore that love. But our prayers seem to hit the ceiling.

Let me add here that my husband has never talked much with his family. He admits he is very independent and says he is not dependent on me or the children for anything.

Last night, after prolonged silence on his part (his way of ignoring us when he is home), he again admitted he had no desire or need to tell us about his day's activities or for us to tell him about our work. He just has no desire for companionship—period.

Now I always had thought that it was a wife's privilege to meet her husband at the door, welcome him home, and share his joys, sorrows, work, children—every aspect of his life. And all these years I've been thrilled to have him around. Perhaps I didn't always show it. Now he says he doesn't want to be kissed and be shown any affection or be talked to. He has always clammed up when we talked about anything controversial.

Now my question is this: I've prayed and prayed, asked forgiveness. How does a woman show love to her husband when he confesses he sometimes doesn't even want to be in the same room with her, doesn't want her love, companionship, or anything else? What do I do? Ignore him? Continue to tell him I love him?

The children are suffering because of this tension in our home, and my heart bleeds for them.

My husband admits that our home is falling apart, but he says he can't do anything about it. And I don't really know if he wants to.

It's hard to understand why your husband is acting as he does and why he would pinpoint his ceasing to love you to a specific period of time—six years ago. It makes me wonder if something in particular happened at that time. For instance, he might have been attracted to someone else and now feels guilt over such attraction.

I wonder if your husband has a romanticized idea of love, and feels that a couple's companionship in marriage and expressions of love should always be the same as when they were first married.

58

I would advise you (if your husband is willing) to seek the help of a Christian psychiatrist or marriage counselor. Such a professional will probe to find the reasons for your husband's withdrawing from you and your children and preferring his own company to that of anyone else.

While I usually advise women (and men) to show their love by their actions and to express love verbally, I would not advise you, in your situation, to force upon your husband any demonstrations of affection. Nor would I advise you to continue to tell him you love him, considering his present attitude toward you. He would only be irritated.

I remember reading in one of Dr. Paul Tournier's books that we cannot *demand* love. After showing love, a person must wait for a response to his love.

No doubt you are constantly wondering, "Why doesn't he love me?" If he hasn't told you why he doesn't love you, don't keep pressing for an answer. But you can ask yourself why. And you can ask God to give you insight to enable you to see any way in which you irritate him, any way in which you have failed him.

One woman who wrote to me about her husband's infidelity told me that after the initial shock and disappointment she was driven to her knees in prayer. She said to God, "Father, I love this man, and I want this marriage to be preserved." Then she, by an effort of the will that had to be repeated again and again, refused to let her thoughts be occupied with finding fault with her husband. Instead, she asked the Lord to show her where *she* had failed as a wife. She spent much time reading the Bible, meditating on it, and waiting on the Lord in prayer. She was renewed spiritually through such quiet times with the Lord.

The restoration of her husband to the Lord and to her

59

didn't take place immediately. After a period of several years he once more became a loving and loyal husband and father.

It isn't easy (in fact, it may be a painful process) for a woman to make the changes in herself that God wants her to make. But her persistence is a proof of the strength of her desire to preserve her marriage, the quality of her love, and her faith in God's active interest in the lives of His children.

Instead of concentrating on your desire to be loved by your husband and to receive expressions of love from him, concentrate on loving him. Ask yourself if you really love him with a love that is greater than romantic love, greater than any human love—the love that is God's kind of love. Examine your life by the phrases in 1 Corinthians 13 that describe this kind of love. Read this chapter every day and ask God to make His love a reality in your life by the power of the Holy Spirit.

Dear Frances,

I am a mother of five children from nineteen months to eight-and-a-half years old. My question is this: How can I get my husband to go out with me and the children for an outing or a picnic? We (my husband, the children, and I) are home most of the time, and I desperately need a change of scene once in a while. But no matter what I say or do my husband says "No," or "I have to rest," or "I've got work to do," or "You go out, and leave the kids to me."

I have gone out alone or with the children many times (and it's hard to drive with five kids in the car). Should I keep going out, with or without the kids, and leave my husband home?

Many other mothers have expressed to me their feeling that they just must get away from confinement to the area

60

within the four walls of their home, so you are not alone in facing such a problem as you describe.

Even though your taking your children with you on a picnic or outing means you still have responsibility for them, such excursions do enable you to experience a change of scene. It would be much more enjoyable, I'm sure, if your husband would go with you and share the responsibility and the fun of giving your children an outing. While you and he will not be free from all difficulties with the children while on an outing, the change will be good for them too and give them experiences which can later be treasured as memories of good times with mother and dad.

The father of a family, because he is with his children fewer hours of the day with the mother, makes quite an impact on their lives. His willingness to take time to have fun with them and to give them his attention can mean a great deal to them—much more than he realizes.

I would advise, "Don't nag your husband about this." Instead, wait for a time when he seems to be in a good mood and when you feel you can control your feelings and talk with him about your desire to have him accompany you and the children on outings. Let him know that you appreciate his willingness to stay at home with the children while you go out alone but that you would enjoy having him with you. Point out that the children would enjoy the companionship of their father on such trips.

Many a man shows a degree of immaturity by his unwillingness to take responsibility as a father. A man will work hard as a wage earner to supply the physical needs of his family, but he may leave his wife almost as alone as a widow in carrying responsibility for bringing up children.

However, a good marriage has a quality of mutuality— mutual love, mutual dependence upon each other, and a mutual adaptability. In addition, a marriage should include a sharing of the responsibility of bringing up the couple's children. I feel sorry for those persons who, when they are grown and think back on their childhood, say, "Our father never did anything *with* us."

If your husband can't see your point, then you will have to accept him as he is, and make plans accordingly. If I were you, I would sometimes go out without him and leave the children in his care. At other times, I would take them along with you.

Dear Frances,

I have never written to anyone for advice in the past, but after listening to your program I am compelled to do so.

I have always thought that home problems could be solved by prayer, reading the Bible, and attendance at our wonderful Bible-centered church. But, Mrs. Nordland, years have gone by and I haven't yet found the answer to my problem, even though I have asked God for help and wisdom in handling the problem of my husband's anger, expressed in unkind words to our children, especially to our thirteen-year-old son Paul. I am so fearful that he will become rebellious and an unhappy adult if things do not change very soon. Whenever Paul doesn't do what he is told, immediately my husband gets very angry and goes on and on.

I have tried to be patient and calm, but my husband insists I am too calm. If I get angry with him, he will blame Paul for upsetting me. My husband has said things that have about broken my heart, such as "I'll leave" and to Paul, "See what you've done now."

I realize that my husband doesn't mean what he says, but the children do not realize this. He doesn't become angry with Jill, our ten-year-old. However, he has never shown much affection to our children. When we were married, I was sure that we could solve any problem with God's help because we were Christians and loved God. Many times I have regretted getting married. My husband will not talk to our pastor, and I am becoming desperate because I haven't been able to find an answer and because of the sadness I see in my son's eyes. Mrs. Nordland, is there an answer to such a problem as this?

I'm sorry for all the unhappiness you have experienced during the years of your marriage. But you are not alone in such unhappiness. Often I have heard women say that you have expressed in your letter: "When I was married, I was sure that we could solve any problem with God's help because we were Christians and loved God."

However, even though the marriage partners are Christians and indwelt by God's Holy Spirit, it's possible for them to "live after the flesh," to use a phrase found in Romans 8. One of the works of the flesh, according to Galatians 5:20, is wrath. That word is rendered "anger" and "ill temper" in some versions. In Ephesians 4:31 the apostle Paul listed wrath and anger as sins which the Christians were to put away.

But it's possible to *know* these things and in your mind approve the things that are right and good and yet be helpless to do what is right and to put out of your life what is wrong. This is the kind of experience described by the apostle Paul in Romans 7, where he said, "to will is present with me; but how to perform that which is good I find not. For the good that I would I do not: but the evil which I would not, that I do" (vv. 18-19). Later (v.24) he exclaimed, "O wretched man that I am! who shall deliver me from the body of this death?" He answered his question with these words: "I thank God [there is deliverance] through Jesus Christ our Lord." But then he added, "So then with the *mind* I myself serve the law of God; but with the flesh the law of sin" (v. 25, italics added).

63

In the next chapter of Romans (chapter 8) we find that the secret of being made free from the law (or principle) of sin which operates in us is another law, another principle: "the law of the Spirit of life in Christ Jesus." Just as engineers have applied the principles of aerodynamics to counteract the principle, or law, of gravity so that a plane weighing many tons can ascend into the air and remain airborne, so the Spirit's law of life in Christ Jesus will counteract the downward pull of the flesh, or the old nature.

It is possible for the believer in Christ to gain victory over anger and to control his temper. But some persons have more of a problem with learning to control their temper because they are naturally of a more volatile temperament. But Christians can *learn* in the sense of *growing* in spiritual maturity. The apostle Paul, in speaking about contentment, said, "I have *learned*." We may fail more often when we are new Christians, but if a person really wants victory he can learn of Christ (Ephesians 4:20-21). But the individual must put his will on the side of God's will, and then depend on Him for strength to do His will.

Some individuals have more difficulty with temper than others do, and may be helped by professional counseling because complex psychological and emotional factors may be involved. If a man has honestly tried to gain victory and has failed again and again, I think he should seek the help of a counselor.

It's unfortunate that your husband refuses to see your pastor. Nowadays most young men who study for the ministry take courses in pastoral psychology and counseling. These, together with their knowledge of the Bible and how to apply its principles to everyday living, equip a pastor for a ministry of counseling his parishioners. But often, in Christian circles, we don't want to take off our masks and let our pastor know how we have failed. We want to give the impression that everything is all right in our home relationship. But putting on a facade is fatal to the kind of relationship with one's pastor that will enable him to help the individual with his problems. Absolute honesty and openness are required. A prerequisite to these qualities is humility—the kind that Jesus referred to when he said, "Except ye be converted, and become as little children, ye shall not enter the kingdom of heaven." Humility is required not only for entering God's spiritual kingdom but also for spiritual growth and progress.

As for yourself, I would advise: Watch your attitudes. Ask yourself, "Am I too critical of my husband?"

Does your statement, "He has never shown much affection to the children," arise out of a critical spirit? Sometimes a woman has a picture in her mind of what her husband should be like in various relationships, and when he doesn't come up to that ideal, she has the feeling that he has let her down as well as their children. But not all men are able to show a great deal of affection to their children. Some men don't relate well to their sons when they are small, and pay little attention to them until they are able to participate in sports and many skills. Often men get along better with their daughters than with their sons, and some women relate better to their sons than to their daughters.

The fact that your husband uses your son as a scapegoat when you are upset shows that your husband is deeply upset about the turmoil caused by his unkind words.

Try to overlook the unkind words. You might say to yourself, "He does love Paul even though he is expressing his anger, frustration, and tensions in this way." Many a married couple have quarreled and said unkind things to each other, but such episodes don't mean that they don't love each other.

65

Make up your mind to refrain from saying anything derogatory about your husband in the presence of the children. You and your husband should not be at odds with one another before your children. When you scold your husband or show anger because of his actions, you are in effect downgrading him and diminishing his authority as head of your home. Of course, I realize that children sometimes need to know that some things are of sufficient importance to parents to warrant their becoming angry. But if the anger is a clean anger which is expressed and the matter that caused the anger isn't brought up again and again, a child will forgive.

Naturally, a child has a hurt look in his eyes when he is reprimanded. Often a child deserves a reprimand. An important principle for parents to remember when they are correcting their children is this: Let what you say be about the *act* not the *person.* Respect your children as persons. Do not label them as stupid, or as thieves or liars, or lazy, or careless. Children are very apt to become discouraged and live up to such labels if constantly applied.

Examine your own attitudes and actions. Pray to God for strength to exercise self-control. At a time when both you and your husband are away from the children and in a calm, relaxed mood, talk with him about this matter that is troubling you. Mention ways in which you have failed, and tell him that you don't want him to think you are being critical for the sake of being critical, but that you are concerned about your son. You might suggest that you pray together aloud about this matter. Many couples don't pray *together* about their failings. Often a wife will say to her husband, "I've been praying for you," and give the impression that this man really needs prayer. He does, but when a wife tells her husband that in a situation like yours, what is said may smack of an attitude of superiority.

Concerning Our Parents

Dear Frances,

I've been experiencing some difficulty in making my mother-in-law really like me. For this reason we don't visit her very often. When we do visit her, if she says something that I don't like, I ignore her.

Since you are a mother-in-law, I thought you could give me some advice. Please tell me some of the things that a mother-in-law might expect from her daughter-in-law.

I think you're making a mistake in trying so hard to "make" your mother-in-law like you. Dr. Paul Tournier points out in one of his books that we cannot demand love. Neither can we demand that various persons like us. Loving and liking must be spontaneous, a response to our personalities as we come in contact with people.

If you treat your mother-in-law as a person of value, significant to you as well as to your husband, and if you shown love by your attitude and actions, I am sure that in time she will respond favorably to you.

Trouble in a strained mother-in-law—daughter-in-law relationship is generated by the fact that the two women both love the same man. But each loves him from a different viewpoint. And often they are jealous of each other's relationship to him.

The mother-in-law, as the older woman, has more experience in life and she should therefore be tolerant with her daughter-in-law if the daughter-in-law is possessive. The older woman would do well to remind herself of the statement in Genesis 2:24, referred to by Jesus in Matthew 19 and Mark 10: "Therefore shall a man leave his father and his mother, and shall cleave unto his wife." If there is any conflict of loyalties after marriage, the young man and the young woman should give preference to the new family unit, not the parental family unit.

What are some of the things a mother-in-law might expect of her daughter-in-law? Well, I cannot speak for all mothers-in-law, but I can tell you what I would like.

1. I would like my son's wife to think of me not so much as a mother-in-law (for the term is one that generates in many women attitudes of hostility, wariness, and jealousy) but as a person who has been deeply involved in her son's life for twenty years or more and therefore continues to love him and to be interested in him. As a person who loves him as a mother, I am not competing with his wife for his affection. I recognize that he loves each of us in a different way.

2. I would like my son's wife to treat me like a friend, giving me the same courtesies she would extend to any friend.

3. I would like my son's wife to treat me as she will want to be treated by her son's wife when he marries.

Dear Frances,

I hope you can help me with a problem I have.

I'm a born-again Christian, living with my husband (who is not born again) and two teenage daughters. My husband is a farmer, and we live on my mother-in-law's farm. We moved here after having lived for nineteen years on a farm in another area. It was the most difficult thing I ever had to do—to leave a large, comfortable home and move into a five-room house only a few feet away from my mother-in-law's home. It was difficult also to leave dear friends and my widowed mother. . . . But my faith that God must have a plan for me kept me going. Sure enough, He put me to work as soon as I got settled. I lead two Bible study groups, and love doing it. I have met many wonderful people since coming here.

Here is my problem: My mother-in-law lives alone in her house. Since moving here I have discovered that she is a very "snoopy" person—downright sneaky, in fact. But what upsets me more than anything else is her listening in on every phone call we get. You see, she is on our line and can hear our ring, for everyone on the line can hear the rings for the parties on that line. We decided to check on her at night, and when I had a call late one evening, my girls ran to see if Grandma was listening—and sure enough, she was. There have been a few times when she has let slip something she has heard by such listening in.

We have all been trying to overlook this, but I'm getting to the place where I find it's difficult to love her and be kind and gracious to her, just because I know she doesn't respect my privacy. My husband won't talk to her about this since he doesn't want to hurt her. Also, we realize she wouldn't talk with us for several weeks if we said something to her about this.

We try very hard to keep an atmosphere of love, but the strain of the situation is telling on me. You see, I really don't think she likes me. She has done several things that I can't understand, and when we visit she clears her throat so often and also scratches herself and pushes at her hair. I take such actions as indications that I make her nervous. She doesn't drive, and I must see to it that she gets to wherever she wants to go. So I invite her to go with me nearly everywhere I go.

Oh, Mrs. Nordland, I have asked God to help me,

and He *has* in many ways. A private line would be the solution, but it would entail extra expense. Also, we would have to pay for putting in the line from the road to our house.

I would appreciate any advice you offer.

Oh, yes, she is a Christian and attends one of the Bible study groups I lead. At these meetings she is very quiet and makes no comments. But sometimes she does so on the way home.

I know it's difficult to give advice when you don't know all the details, but I have written to you because I feel I cannot continue to go on ignoring something that gotten to me.

I take it that your telephone line is one on which you can tell if someone else on the line is listening. It could be that at times persons other than your mother-in-law might be listening. But, of course, you know from sending your daughters to "spy" on Grandma, that she was listening on one particular occasion. And you have concluded, from her conversations, that she has listened at other times.

Though you state that a private line would be a solution, I am wondering if it would be. It's true that your having a private line would remove the irritation you feel because you suspect that she is listening to your phone conversations. But she would not be changed as a person, nor would you be. I realize you resent the intrusion into your privacy, but are you certain that having a private line would eliminate your resentful feelings? You speak of her as being "snoopy" and "downright sneaky." Does this description of her apply to other matters? If so, then you will have to overcome your resentment about such flaws in her character.

Have you ever asked yourself why she listens in? Perhaps her life is rather dull and routine, with not much happening that is interesting and exciting. Now, when I ask you to

70

consider this aspect, I'm not condoning her actions, for it is as improper to listen in on the conversations of others as it is dishonorable to read letters addressed to another person.

If you consider why she does it, perhaps you can be "big enough" to laugh it off with a comment something like this: "Well, if my phone conversations entertain her, I won't stew about her listening in!"

Of course, you could confront her with your knowledge of what she has been doing, but she would be terribly hurt, which, of course, would run counter to your husband's desires. And you should consider his desires since she is *his* mother.

Another way of handling the situation is to make up your mind that you won't talk about anything on the phone that you would not want to share with her. Perhaps you could neutralize her snoopiness by sharing more of your family happenings with her, more of your plans, more of your thoughts. Oh, I know you don't *have* to. But doing more than you have to is like going the "second mile"; it's a gratuitous thing to do. It's giving something of yourself. And to give is more blessed than to receive, according to the teaching of Jesus.

I think the expression in 1 Peter 4:8, "Charity [love] shall cover the multitude of sins" would apply to this situation. While love doesn't condone sin, it may choose to refrain from exposing someone else's sins or faults.

It seems to me that part of your problem was your reluctance to live close to your mother-in-law when you moved. I noticed from your letter that you not only mentioned that it was difficult for you to leave a large, comfortable home to move to a five-room house but that you added "only a few feet away from my mother-in-law's home."

I would advise that, as you think about your feelings

71

about your mother-in-law, you go beyond the particular problem of her intrusion into your privacy to an examination of your entire relationship with her.

Accept her as she is. We meet with so many feelings of frustration when we try to change individuals, especially older persons. Forgive her for those qualities in her which irritate you. If you truly forgive, you won't have resentment. Forgiveness on our part should be patterned after God's forgiveness of us. We have offended Him and sinned against Him in many ways, and yet He freely forgives us. And when He forgives, He forgets. I know that it's impossible for us to "forget" in the sense of being unable to recall certain incidents, but we can control our thoughts in this way: When the resentful feelings rise within you, deliberately, by an act of the will, turn your thinking to other channels. Make this as definite an act as when turning a knob on your television set or your radio to tune in another station and thus change programs.

Yield yourself to God, asking Him to take over in every area of your life so that the Holy Spirit, ungrieved by resentful feelings and lack of forgiveness, will be able to produce in you the fruit of the Spirit, which includes love. Examine daily your attitudes and action by the decription of love given in 1 Corinthians 13, and ask God to enable you to love your mother-in-law in that way. *You* cannot do it, as you have discovered, but *God* can.

A saying I have found helpful in controlling a resentful feeling is one I discovered in one of Amy Carmichael's books. She related how she was disturbed about something, and it kept bothering her while she was riding a train in India. Then the rhythm of the wheels on the tracks seemed to beat out repeatedly words that were like a mesage from God: "Let it be, think of Me. Let it be, think of Me."

Dear Frances,

I am a single woman forty-eight years old. I live in a nice house with my seventy-seven-year-old father who is a semi-invalid. He uses crutches but is able to be left alone and help himself while I am at work. My mother, who was an invalid for twenty-five years, died several years ago.

This is my problem: All the rest of my family seem to think my father is my responsibility, not theirs. My family includes a brother who lives about seventy-five miles away, two married sisters, and one divorced sister.

So completely does my family leave the responsibility of my father to me that they didn't even care for him when I had to be in a hospital for a week on two different occasions. It was necessary for me to prepare my father's meals in advance because my sisters and brother didn't offer to come and get my father and take him to one of their homes. Neither did they prepare any food and bring it to him. All they were interested in was when I would be home.

I had an argument on the phone with my sister when I asked her if she couldn't come and get father one Sunday while I was away. She replied that she had her own family to spend Sunday with. She also said, "After all, he lives with *you*." And I replied, "He is your father, too."

Some of the excuses they have for not taking father for a week or so are: "He would make me nervous." "I don't have room." "I work all the time."

When it is their vacation time, they just pack up and go, and while they are away they send a card telling what a good time they are having. I just finished a vacation and didn't even get to go out of town for a weekend.

I pay for all my father's needs beyond his $120-a-month social security check.

For a brief period (four months) my father was in

an old people's home, but the staff couldn't tolerate him because of his behavior. Not all the people there were strangers to him, for he knew a good many people that resided there.

I must admit that my father does many things that aggravate me. I have no inclination to entertain friends because my father dominates the conversation, speaking mainly of himself. He has a nice room but only uses it for sleeping. His friends have all deserted him, as he says things that people resent. For instance, he told several people that he was sure my mother wasn't a Christian when she passed away, so he is certain she didn't go to heaven. He claims he is a good Christian, and yet he says things like that! He is very ungrateful, too. He thinks the world owes him everything.

I will close now, hoping to hear from you soon as to what advice you can give.

What advice can I give you? Advice is easy to give. One of my radio listeners (who was a bit bitter, in my opinon) said, "It's easy to preach; harder to do."

We should be slow to offer advice when it isn't requested. But when it is asked for, as in your case, then the counselor needs to try to put herself in the skin of the other person.

I do not envy you your position one bit.

I am wondering if the personality characteristics you describe have been apparent throughout your father's adult life or just in recent years. If they have been more noticeable in recent years, it may be that they are intensified because of old age. I recall a meditation on old age written by Dr. Richard Halvorsen in which he said, "Take note of the old man on the path ahead of you, for some day *you* will be that old man." He emphasized that we are *becoming* what we will *be.* All of us need to be alert lest we allow

74

ourselves to become self-pitying, sour, grumpy, hard-to-get-along-with old men and women.

Even though you recognize the emotional changes in your father through waning of his physical and mental powers, through loss of status when he was no longer able to support and care for himself, and through missing the companionship of his wife, it is not likely that he will change at the age of seventy-seven. He is what he has been becoming. You will need to accept him as he is—and love him. You may not *like* what he is, but as you seek to fulfill God's command for Christians to love one another and His command for children to honor their parents, you will enter in a new way, I believe, into the quality of God's love. God's kind of love is constant and unconditional. God may not always approve of our conduct, but He always loves us. And he is full of compassion as He observes our weaknesses and failures.

You also need God's power to enable you to love as He would have you love your brother and your sisters while they selfishly go their own ways, with no interest in helping you bear the burden of caring for your father. It's easy to feel resentful when others don't do their part. We say it isn't fair. But nowhere in the Bible are we told that we will get fair treatment in this world. When people aren't fair in their treatment of us, we are not responsible for *their* actions and attitudes. However, we are responsible for our own.

Even though I have mentioned first *your* attitudes, I would also suggest these practical approaches: Insist on a meeting of all your family (your brother and three sisters) at which you will initiate a discussion of ways in which they could help you share the responsibility of caring for your father. I think any counselor would say that you should have relief once in a while to go on a vacation, to go away for a weekend every now and then.

I think you will be better able to put up with your father's idiosyncrasies if you can be relieved of your responsibility for short periods. Everyone performs his work better for having had a vacation, and you need periodic vacations from your father. If your brother and sisters care for your father now and then, they will more greatly appreciate what you are doing by making a home for him. It may be that your father's disposition will improve if he has a vacation from you, if he has the change he will experience by being in the home of another member of his family.

At the family get-together which I have suggested (if you are able to arrange it), you might point out to your brother and sisters the possibility that their children may some day disclaim all responsibility for caring for them as a result of seeing their parents' indifference and lack of concern for their aged, crippled father. Example is a powerful teacher.

Another suggestion: Try to get your father into another old people's home, if at all possible. If you gain admittance for him, you will need to talk to him sternly and firmly about his conduct. Tell him that we repel people who might be our friends if we are highly critical, overtalkative, and self-centered. On the other hand, we can attract people to us if we are interested in them, are good listeners, and are amiable in disposition.

If, after all your efforts to make some changes in your situation, you are unsuccessful, then you will have to accept your circumstances as the circumstances of God's choice for you and trust Him to give you strength to be patient, loving, and kind, and to triumph over the resentment that is bound to well up in you now and then just because you are human.

I can't help but think of this statement made by a young man whose life plans had been drastically changed because of serious wounds received while he was in Vietnam: "Well, if I can't do what I *want* to do, then I'll simply do what I *have* to do."

In Times of Loneliness

Dear Frances,
  I have been widowed recently, and since you have had the experience of being a widow, I am writing to ask you: Does one ever get over this loneliness?

Yes, you can get over the loneliness that an individual feels when, after long years of marriage, his mate is taken home to heaven.

Of course, getting over the loneliness will depend not only on the factor of time but upon your attitude. For instance, a widow with whom I talked when I was visiting in Denver said to me, "For a long time after my husband's death I just wallowed in self pity."

You can live life in a self-centered sort of way, turning your thoughts inward—to "poor me." Or you can learn to accept the bereavement as allowed of God and, therefore, in His will for you. Since God is continuing to give you life and strength, He certainly has a purpose in keeping you here. Find out what He wants you to do with your life.

Someone has said, "The best way to cure your loneliness is to look for someone more lonely than yourself." It's in seeking to help others that we will find healing for ourselves. I found this to be true in my own experience as a widow.

Overcoming loneliness doesn't mean that you must

cease to think of the one who has been your companion for so many years. It's only normal to think of him. The way an individual feels when he is first bereaved has been described as an emotional amputation. It hurts! And it takes time for the hurt to heal. Even though we say that *God* is the healer of broken hearts, yet we need to recognize that the healing process takes time.

Each person needs to work through his own grief. No one else can do it for him. However, the person who is a Christian does not face working through his grief alone. God is with him, and he has the comfort of the promises of the Word of God—promises about God's all-sufficient grace, the realities of the resurrection of the body and of that heavenly home which Jesus called "my Father's house."

Dear Frances,
   I am a widow, fifty-one years old. I lost my husband almost four years ago. We had been married for thirty-one years, and if it had not been for the Lord I could not have made it thus far. . . . I am so lonely now. . . . Here is my question: Is it right for me to pray for a companion?

It certainly isn't wrong for a Christian woman to pray for God to give her a companion, for God has told us (through the apostle Paul in Philippians 4:6-7), "Be careful [anxious] for nothing; but in every thing by prayer and supplication with thanksgiving let your requests be made known unto God. And the peace of God, which passeth all understanding, shall keep your hearts and minds through Christ Jesus."

Since the Lord is interested in every phase of your life because you are His child, you may be confident of His interest in your desire for a companion. He comforted you in your sorrow, and He understands your loneliness.

But when you pray to God about this matter, you must remember that there are many other women praying for a husband, too. And not all of them will have their prayers answered positively. If you were to consider the statistics, the ratio of available eligible men to the number of women who are single or widows, you would see that there just are not enough men. If I remember the figures which I read a few years ago, they were something like this: In the age bracket between fifty and sixty-five, there were fifteen women to each man. Then when you consider that not all these men are desirable from the viewpoint of the Christian, you can see why it is that *so many* Christian *women* who are widows do not marry again. The Christian woman, if she follows the teaching of the Bible, will not marry a man who is not a Christian, or one who has been divorced. And the woman who is spiritually mature may not want to marry a man who is a Christian but spiritually immature. Of course, numerous other factors should be considered by the individual who is contemplating entering a relationship as intimate as marriage.

Dr. Paul Tournier, in his book *Escape from Loneliness,* says that the Christian answer for both women and men is to surrender their love destiny into the hands of God. And he suggests praying something like this:

> O God, this instinct which thou hast given me—I offer it up in turn to thee. Direct my life according to thy good pleasure and thine infinite wisdom. If thou art pleased to give me a husband, as I so desire, I want to receive one only as from thee. Even then, keep me from using my instinct for other purposes than for what thou dost want—for my own enjoyment rather than for the fulfilling of thy will for me. If it please thee to keep me single, grant me the grace to accept it with all my heart and to know that my

life can be happy and beautiful only if it is according to thy will.[1]

Dr. Tournier says, "There is no inner conflict and no repression of desire in such an attitude of surrender, providing it is sincere and deep, and an integral part of one's total consecration. There is neither a deceitful denial of one's desire to marry nor any denial of the sexual drive itself; neither is there any tension because of the desire."[2]

Shortly after I married the second time, a woman came to chat with me at a Bible conference I was attending. She said, "I'm glad you married again. It's so lonely living alone." I replied, "I would not have married just baceuse I was lonely. I married because I felt this was God's will for me and because I respected, admired, and loved this man." And I recalled something written by psychologist Erich Fromm to the effect that the best marriages are those which are not based on a neurotic need.

To marry out of loneliness is unwise. To marry because of God's guidance to that decision is wise, and the two partners can expect God's blessing upon their lives as together they walk with God and seek to please Him.

In the decision to marry, as well as in other important decisions of life, it is well to remember what is written in Proverbs 3:5-6: "Trust in the Lord with all thine heart; and lean not unto thine own understanding. In all thy ways acknowledge him, and he shall direct thy paths."

Dear Frances,

I'm a high school teacher. I've taught six classes today—and for what? I'm finishing a thesis at Ohio State University—and for what? In the ten years and more that I have taught, I have wanted a husband

---

1. From ESCAPE FROM LONELINESS, by Paul Tournier. Copyright © MCMLXII, W. L. Jenkins. Used by permission of the Westminster Press.
2. Ibid.

and a family. As I sit here alone in a nicely furnished apartment, I ought to be thankful to the Lord for all He has given me, which is much.

But how can I keep saying to myself, *The Lord answers prayer; the Lord meets our needs,* when the only men who ask me for dates are non-Christian men? After a few evenings with such men and saying, "No, I don't drink; no, I don't dance," I say to them, "I don't think it's fair for me to date you anymore because, you see, I have accepted Jesus Christ as my Saviour. And the Bible says that a believer in Jesus Christ should not be united with an unbeliever." Of course, such situations give me an opportunity for testimony, and sometimes the gentleman will attend church services with me.

About three years ago I thought the Bible verse that says "If we ask any thing according to his will, he heareth us" meant that if I asked God to bring to a decision to accept Christ a man I was dating whom I liked very much, He would, because it is not His will that "any should perish." The man with whom I was keeping company then asked me to marry him, but I had to say no; and after praying about it, I felt God would not have me date him anymore because I could not become engaged to him. I couldn't get away from the Bible verse, "Be ye not unequally yoked together with unbelievers."

Since Sunday school days I've been taught: God has a plan for your life; He has a mate for you; pray about it; let Him have His way in your life.

Is the longing for a home and children a need? If so, I can rely on God's promise to supply all our needs. Or is this longing only a desire which I should commit to God to fill—or not to fill, as He sees fit?

I'm afraid to stop asking because several books on prayer say something like this: "If we could only see all that God had willed for us that we never claimed."

83

And the authors refer to the verse in James: "Ye have
not because ye ask not."

The longing for a mate is a natural and normal desire.
Psychologists may speak of it as a need, but I don't think
it is what can be described as an imperative need—like
our need for water and food. If these needs were not met,
we would eventually die. But without a mate you can live;
perhaps you would call it merely existing. Many women,
however, have learned to accept their single state and have
found many satisfactions in life. It is called sublimation
when a woman channels the love that she would have
invested in homemaking and in loving and caring for
a husband and children to other lives. She can do this
in the professions of teaching and nursing, in Sunday
school teaching, through volunteer service in children's
hospitals or in a ministry to the aged, to shut-ins, to those
who are handicapped.

I think you can honestly bring your longing for a mate
to the Lord and pour out your heart before Him, telling
Him just how you feel, with the confidence that He cares
about you, and He understands your longing. But this is
something that a yielded Christian will commit to the Lord,
the sovereign Ruler of our lives and of the universe. And
it may be that He will yet fulfill your desire for a mate.
It isn't for you to tell God when. God is never behind
time or ahead of time. He is the One who worketh all
things "according to the good pleasure of his will" (Ephesians 1:5).

It's true that when we pray for someone to be saved,
our prayer is an appropriate one. In the Bible we have
the example of the apostle Paul who said, "My heart's
desire and prayer to God for Israel is, that they might
be saved" (Romans 10:1). But not all Israel of Paul's
generation were saved. Only a few were saved.

The Scripture that describes the Lord as being "long-suffering, . . . not willing that any should perish, but that all should come to repentance" (2 Peter 3:9) has been translated in the New American Standard Version this way: "not wishing for any to perish but for all to come to repentance." Kenneth Wuest, teacher of New Testament Greek at the Moody Bible Institute for many years, said, in commenting on this verse, "It is not God's considered will that any should perish. There is the sovereignty of God and the free will of man. God will not violate man's will. While it is His considered will that no one should be lost, yet in making man in His image He necessarily had to make him a free moral agent, with a will which is able to say 'yes' and 'no' to Him. While God is always willing to save man, man is not always willing to be saved."[1]

It may be that the man for whom you have prayed will yet be saved. I wonder if you still pray for him to be saved, even though you aren't dating him?

A point to consider when thinking about apparently unanswered prayer that God will give you a husband is this: In a monogamous society, we cannot expect that every woman will find a mate. Statistics are my basis for saying this. A few years ago financial columnist Sylvia Porter predicted that in 1965 we would be entering the era of the forlorn maidens. She said this would be the year when the total of girls reaching marriage age would start to outnumber by hundreds of thousands the total of boys of marriage age, that is, boys a few years older than the girls they would marry.

The teaching you received in your Sunday school to the effect that God has a mate for everyone was not based on Scripture, so don't blame God because He hasn't sent you a mate. I think it would be far better to give to young

---

1. *In These Last Days* (Grand Rapids: Eerdmans, 1957), p. 71. Used by permission of the publisher.

people the concept that God has a plan for every life and that each person will find the greatest happiness and deepest contentment as he commits his way unto the Lord.

Next, we ought not to consider prayer primarily as a way of getting things for ourselves. Just because I'm a Christian, I shouldn't expect to be spared the common sufferings of mankind. And one of those sufferings—until you adjust to your single state—is loneliness. A person with an immature faith expects to get private miracles, expects God to treat him as a pet, a pampered child. A person with mature faith expects to get private miracles, expects God an opportunity to worship Him, thank Him, praise Him, and present petitions to Him. As we present our petitions to God, it is appropriate that we subordinate our desires to His will. We will find our greatest happiness as we choose to live in harmony with His will.

Due to Divorce

Dear Frances,

I've just been listening to you on the radio. When you asked, "Are you discouraged?" my reaction was: "This is one morning when I am more than discouraged."

I am a grandmother, sixty years old.

My divorced son and his eleven-year-old daughter are staying in our home. My son works at two jobs. He works four hours in the daytime, and nine to ten hours at night. He sleeps during the day (short naps). He's had one heart attack, and the doctor told him to slow down.

So he has no time for his daughter. When he is home, he's really too tired to listen to her and talk to her. This girl goes to see her mother every other week (if the mother wants her). So we have a nervous, high-strung girl who is terribly unhappy. She is failing in school, and is very quiet and withdrawn— not at all like she was when her parents were together. Her mother openly lives with a man.

I've prayed for all of them. So far our granddaughter continues to be upset, and we are, too. My husband works long hours as a night watchman, so he sleeps most of the day.

How can I go along without getting involved emotionally, since we love our granddaughter and our son?

Part of the tragedy of divorce is the pain the children suffer. Most youngsters find it extremely difficult to accept the idea of their parents getting a divorce or the finality of it, once the divorce is granted. Many children continue to hope for a reuniting of their parents, and thus postpone their own adjustment to the situation.

No wonder your granddaughter is unhappy! She is grieving over the separation of her parents, both of whom she loves. Perhaps she is also grieving over the unpleasantness that occurred before the divorce, for in such situations, the divorce is not what broke up the marriage but the inability to get along, the lack of love and consideration, or, in some cases, the infidelity of one of the marriage partners. And now this little girl knows that her mother is living with a man to whom she is not married.

No wonder she is quiet and withdrawn. No wonder it is difficult for her to concentrate on her school work. She has much to think about. And she will have to work through her grief, just as an older person who is bereaved (or even a child who is bereaved) must work through his grief.

Give her all the love you can. Urge her father to give her as much time and attention as he can. This will let her know that he loves her. Perhaps he is working as much as he does because work represents a form of escape from his private grief over the failure of his marriage.

Don't criticize either parent. Don't poison the child's mind against either her father or her mother by discussing his or her shortcomings.

I would suggest that you refrain from prying into the girl's thoughts and feelings. On the other hand, be ready to listen sympathetically if she should open up and express how she feels. Suggest that she bring a friend home from school whenever the fancy strikes her. Urge her to develop friendships with the girls of her Sunday school class, and

tell her to feel free to invite any of them to come home
with her to your house on the weekends when she isn't
visiting her mother.

You can't avoid being involved emotionally. But your
emotional involvement can put an "O God" element in
your prayers as you pray for all concerned and work for
the spiritual well-being, health, and happiness of your
granddaughter.

Dear Frances,

I am a widow, and eight months ago I met a man
who was divorced from his wife. He was not a Christian, but two months ago while we attended an evangelistic meeting he accepted the Lord.

He says there is no chance of a reconciliation with
his former wife. Can we marry without going contrary
to the teaching of the Bible? I realize I should not be
led by sentiment, but I love him very much and we
seem so right together.

I can find in the Bible only one valid reason for divorce
—a marriage partner's unfaithfulness.

Not all marriage partners who go through the difficult
experience of discovering infidelity to the marriage vows
sue for divorce. Some choose to forgive and remain with
the offending party.

Regarding marriage after divorce, some Bible teachers
are of the opinion that even though there is a valid reason
for divorce (infidelity), and a divorce decree is obtained,
the innocent party should not marry while the other party
is living. These teachers believe that death alone severs
the marriage relationship. Others believe that where there
is a valid reason for divorce remarriage is allowable.

If you will look up and read Matthew 19:3-9, you will
find Jesus' teaching about divorce. In that passage we find
that He called the attention of the Pharisees to the fact

that God's ideal is for a man and a woman to view marriage as a permanent union, even though Moses' law permitted Hebrew men (because of the hardness of their hearts) to put away their wives. (See Deuteronomy 24:1-4.)

Matthew 19:9 would apply particularly to your question: "And I say unto you, Whosoever shall put away his wife, except it be for fornication, and shall marry another, committeth adultery: and whoso marrieth her which is put away doth commit adultery."

I realize there are those who would say that since the man you refer to was divorced when he was a non-Christian that what is past is "under the blood of Christ" and therefore forgiven. That's true concerning a persons *sins*. But some things that were done before a person's conversion can be made right after his conversion. For instance, many individuals have made restitution of stolen goods or money after conversion. And some broken marriages can be restored after conversion.

We need to consider that marriage was ordained of God as part of His government of the human race. So the marriage law applies to all people, whether they are Christians or not.

When a man who is married becomes a Christian and his past is viewed as "under the blood of Christ," this does not cancel his marriage and his responsibility to his wife and children. In 1 Corinthians 7, the apostle Paul gave this instruction for a person who had become a believer and whose spouse was not a Christian: "And unto the married I command . . . Let not the wife depart from her husband: But . . . if she depart, let her remain unmarried, or be reconciled to her husband: and let not the husband put away his wife. . . . If any brother hath a wife that believeth not, and she be pleased to dwell with him, let him not put her away. And the woman which hath an husband that believeth not, and if he be pleased to dwell with her, let her not leave him." From this section of Scripture we see that Paul urged husbands and wives to stay togeher, even though only one was a believer. Also that, if a wife were to depart from her husband, she was to remain unmarried or be reconciled to her husband.

If we were to apply this instruction to a situation where a man had been divorced before his conversion and his wife had not married again, it would seem that he should remain unmarried or seek a reconciliation with his wife.

You do not mention the reason for your friend's divorce. If the reason was incompatibility, might he not find, now that he is a Christian, the ability to live with and love his former wife and win her to faith in the Lord Jesus?

How can you be sure that part of the difficulty in his marriage did not lie with him? How can you be sure, if you were to marry him, that you and he would have a good marriage? After all, you have not known him very long, and he has been a Christian only two months. Marriage counselors say that usually, when a divorced person marries again, he brings part of the problems of the first marriage (himself) into the second marriage.

It's easy when you're alone, after having experienced the companionship of a marriage that was terminted by the death of your husband, to let your heart go out in affection to a man who shows his interest in you. But as you go through life and are confronted with important decisions, there are times when you must let your head rule instead of your heart.

I would advise: Follow God's will for you, even though it means saying no to your desire to marry this man. Trust God to guide you into a marriage that will not violate scriptural principles. And ask God to enable you to accept the possibility that it may be His will for you to remain alone. Only in accepting His will with all your heart will you find peace.

Because of Death

Dear Frances,
Our dear eighteen-year-old grandson Joe, who was a jungle fighter, was killed in Vietnam. Prior to his death I had put so much faith in prayer, and my every thought of him was a prayer for his safety and the safety of his buddies. Four ministers who knew Joe and three prayer groups said they also were praying for him. I had his picture in my Bible at the Ninety-first Psalm, which I read each day. Also, I pinned my faith to the promise, "If ye shall ask any thing in my name, I will do it" (John 14:14). I asked God many times, day and night, to protect Joe and bring him safely home after his time was up.

Now I am confused about how to pray. Can you help me?

Joe knew the Lord, and was planning to go to college after he completed his military service. We shall always miss him.

I feel deeply for you and for all parents and grandparents who have suffered a bereavement like yours. When we who are Christians go through such heartache, we are one with the whole creation, which "groaneth and travaileth in pain together," as we wait for the time of redemption when Christ will come again and the time when He will rule in righteousness on the earth and the nations will no longer make war against each other. The reason the world will then experience peace will be because of a government that will be administered in righteousness by the Prince of Peace.

But until that time, those who die believing in the Lord go immediately into the presence of the Lord in heaven, where there is no sin, no warfare, no sorrow, no suffering, sickness, death nor tears. The chief comfort of those who have been bereaved is to know that the loved one who has died as a believer is in heaven, in the presence of the Lord who loved us and gave Himself for us. And all the bereaved who are believers have the hope of seeing their loved ones again some day.

According to 1 Thessalonians 4, it is the truth about the resurrection and the return of our Lord Jesus Christ that is to be the Christian's source of comfort. The apostle Paul wrote, "Wherefore comfort one another with these words."

In addition to those words in 1 Thessalonians 4:13-18, we can find other words, or phrases, in the New Testament which will comfort us.

For instance, it's precious to know that God is described as "the God of all comfort, who comforteth us in all our tribulation" (2 Corinthians 1:3-4).

Jesus, knowing that His disciples would experience sorrow because of His death and His departure from them, said, "Let not your heart be troubled: ye believe in God, believe also in me. In my Father's house are many mansions: if it were not so, I would have told you. I go to prepare a place for you" (John 14:1-2).

In 2 Corinthians 5 the apostle Paul wrote about his willingness to be absent from the body because absence from the body would mean being present with the Lord. To be with the Lord in heaven is an experience far better than the best that life on this earth can offer.

However, the strongest instinct with which God has

endowed man is the instinct to live, to survive. I'm certain your grandson wanted to live. And you and others wanted him to live too.

I have grandsons who may at some time in the future go into military service. And if they do, I will pray for them each day. How will I pray for them? Of course, I will pray for their physical safety, but I will add this phrase to my prayers, "If it be Thy will."

I cannot find in the Bible any promise made to Christians that grants them exemption from the trials of life. Christians as well as non-Christians get sick; Christians as well as non-Christians will someday die (except for that generation of Christians who will be living when the Lord Jesus Christ returns). Some Christian soldiers as well as some non-Christian soldiers are wounded while they are engaged in warfare, and some Christian soldiers as well as some non-Christian soldiers will die as the result of enemy action.

I realize that many people, like yourself, have rested on the promises found in Psalm 91. However, I do not believe that Christians should claim these promises, which were made (as some Bible teachers have taught) to the coming Messiah. Two verses of this psalm (verses 11 and 12) were applied by Satan to Jesus during the temptation in the wilderness, without any contradiction by Jesus. I do not believe that promises we read in the Bible that were made to specific individuals facing a specific situation can be claimed by individuals today. Of course, as we read the Old Testament and observe God's dealings with individuals, we can learn certain timeless principles that we can apply in our lives. A good example is a phrase spoken to Eli by an unkown prophet: "Them that honour me I will honour" (1 Samuel 2:30).

As we read the Old Testament, we can learn much about God's character that will encourage us to trust in Him no matter what our circumstances are. He is trustworthy; we can rely on Him because of His great faithfulness. His love is steadfast. He has compassion on His people in all their trials and sufferings. He is slow to anger, and He is longsuffering. He is righteous. Because He is righteous, we can have the same confidence Abraham had when he and God were talking about the impending destruction of Sodom and Gomorrah—the confidence that the Judge of all the earth would do right. (See Genesis 18:25.)

Even though I believe that the promises made in Psalm 91 should not be claimed by Christians today, I am persuaded that present-day believers are more privileged than were the believers of Old Testament times. We have the Bible in our homes. We have the entire Bible, the New Testament as well as the Old Testament. We have in the New Testament the revelation of God's love in His Son Jesus Christ; and the gospel, the good news that whoever believes in Jesus Christ will not perish but have everlasting life, is plainly stated. Furthermore, we are told in Romans 8 that nothing can separate believers from the love of God in Christ—neither life nor death, nor angels, nor principalities, nor powers, nor things present, nor things to come.

In Romans 8, I see quite a contrast to Psalm 91. In Romans 8 the apostle Paul, as he wrote, faced the very real possibility of tribulation, distress, persecution, famine, nakedness, peril, and sword (warfare), and then he quoted a verse from Psalm 44: "For thy sake we are killed all the day long; we are accounted as sheep for the slaughter." Following that quotation he expressed his confidence in God: "In all these things we are more than conquerors through him that loved us." But in Psalm 91, the writer of the psalm, inspired by the Holy Spirit, says to an unnamed individual (whom some believe to be the Messiah),

"He shall cover thee with his feather, and under his wings shalt thou trust. . . . Thou shalt not be afraid for the terror by night; nor for the arrow that flieth by day; nor for the pestilence that walketh in darkness; nor for the destruction that wasteth at noonday." It seems that these verse describe warfare and an epidemic of illness—perhaps a plague. The writer, after describing these conditions, said, "A thousand shall fall at thy side, and ten thousand at thy right hand; but it shall not come nigh thee."

If that verse applied to all believers in all the centuries of history, then God was not faithful to His promises. What an awful indictment of God! Instead, we ought to say with the apostle Paul, "Let God be true, but every man a liar" (Romans 3:4). God is faithful, trustworthy, dependable, and reliable. If ever it seems to us that God has failed in keeping His promises, then we must say, "We have failed in interpreting these Scriptures when applying them to ourselves."

If it seems that God has failed in keeping His promises, we must remind ourselves that God is omnipotent. Since this is so, it follows that if the loved one we prayed for was killed in battle, it was not because God was not able to keep him from death. Nothing is beyond God's power. However, even though God is almighty, He limits Himself. In His sovereignty and perfect wisdom, He chooses to do thus and so, or He chooses not to. But always He loves us.

We need to consider this too: God has not created men as automatons; He allows men to make choices that affect the course of history. Then too, certain laws operate in the universe, such as the law of gravity and the law of cause and effect.

Even though we consider all these, we recognize that God is sovereign. We cannot put God in a box and limit Him by our concepts of Him. But we can trust Him, and love and serve Him, and wait for that day when the things we don't understand now, which cause us such heartache, will be made plain.

Regarding the verse, "If ye shall ask anything in my name, I will do it" (John 14:14), I would say that asking in Christ's name is the key to understanding this verse. If you ask in His name, you will not ask for anything that is contrary to His will.

Dear Frances,

I listen to you every day. . . . I have kept putting off writing to you, but something within me keeps urging me to write to you. I don't really know how anyone but God can help me—and perhaps I don't deserve any help.

Some months ago my eldest son died as a result of head injuries he received in an automobile accident. The boy who was driving the car was dead when others arrived at the scene. Since my son survived the accident, even though his condition was listed as critical, I took this as an indication that he was to have another chance at life. I prayed almost without ceasing; and when my son's condition changed from critical to serious and then to fair in a matter of three days, I was persuaded that God had had a hand in his improvement. The doctors had told us he had one chance in a million to live.

When our son recovered consciousness, he was in terrible pain until sedatives were given after the doctors felt it was safe to do so. Much of the time we were at the hospital he rested; and as the time drew near for him to be given a pill, he was usually begging for it, as his head hurt him so.

Now the reason I have told you all this is perhaps because I am trying to excuse myself for failing to speak to my son about his soul's welfare and failing to try to help him get ready to meet God. I was praying so for his healing; and when he seemed to improve, I felt I would have time when he felt better to talk to him about his soul. I had spoken to him many times about this important matter at home when he was well but not after the accident. I had thought, by all reports, that he was improving, but then one night a call came from the hospital informing us that he had gone into a coma. Then I tried to intercede to God about his soul, but I was raised to believe that we could not do this for anyone, though we could pray for their healing. I never had another chance to talk with him, for he lived only two-and-a-half days after that, all the while in a coma.

I had been so afraid to talk to him about how bad his condition was; and I felt that, if I talked to him about his soul, he would think he was going to die.

I could hardly accept his death at first. Then one day my husband asked me how I had prayed for our son's healing. I told him that when I prayed I added the words, "If it be Thy will." My husband then told me I must accept our son's death as God's will.

One day when I was pondering over this heartache, I read John 3:16: "For God so loved the world, that he gave his only begotten Son, that whosoever believeth in him should not perish, but have everlasting life." I felt much better for a time, but the guilt is here with me most of the time.

As I read your letter, my heart ached for you. It may be true, as you mention, that no one but God can help you. But God sometimes helps us in our griefs and sorrows through our friends who are His servants. This was true in the experience of the apostle Paul. He wrote in 2 Corinthians 7:6: "Nevertheless God, that comforteth those that are cast down [or discouraged], comforted us by the coming of Titus."

I would also call your attention to this verse: "God

is our refuge and strength, a very present help in trouble" (Psalm 46:1). This period of your life, since the death of your son, has been a time of trouble, of deep grief. And you must believe that God is present with you as a help. He loves you; He is interested in you right now. He knows about your guilt feelings. He knows too, as you do, that what is past cannot be undone.

If you feel that you have sinned against your son and against God is not witnessing to your son after he was injured, your only course is this: to believe what God has said in 1 John 1:9: "If we confess our sins, he is faithful and just to forgive us our sins, and to cleanse us from all unrighteousness." God's grace is greater than the greatest of sins. The apostle Paul considered himself the chief of sinners (1 Timothy 1:15); he knew he was responsible for the deaths of some of the early Christians. Yet he believed that God had forgiven him. And he realized that he had a life to live, a race to run, and work to do for the Lord until the Lord called him home to heaven.

I am glad that you spoke to your son many times about his relationship to the Lord when he was well and at home. In my opinion, the time when we should talk to non-Christians about the Lord is when they are well. We ought not wait until a person is ill. Often a person who has been injured or is very ill cannot think clearly (because of his pain or physical weakness or the effects of sedatives) and make a response to what is said to him about God's love and His free gift of eternal life, offered to all who will believe on His Son Jesus Christ.

I remember a fine Christian woman who was very ill with pneumonia. My first husband was her pastor and paid her a pastoral visit in the hospital. Later she said, "You know, people ought not to wait until someone is seriously ill before talking to that one about the Lord. I was so ill that, had I been an unsaved person, I could not have made a decision; in fact, I wouldn't have cared. All I wanted to do was to die and be released from my physical misery. It didn't matter to me that a minister was there in my hospital room."

I can see how you feel about not wanting to give your son the impression that he was near death. Naturally, it would seem that that was an inappropriate time to speak to him. But the apostle Paul told Timothy, a young pastor, to "preach the word . . . in season, out of season." William F. Beck's translation renders this verse (2 Timothy 4:2) this way: "Preach the Word, keep at it at the right time and the wrong time."[1] If you had spoken to your son when he was so ill, he might have accepted the Lord, and then again he might not have done so. At least, if you had spoken to him, you would not be under the burden of guilt you now feel because you failed to speak to him at that time.

I would advise you to recall that your son had heard about Christ through you earlier, as well as in church and Sunday school. It could be that he did make a decision for the Lord without having told you about it. He could have made such a decision during moments of consciousness in the hospital, and he may have been reluctant to say anything about it to you. Often there are barriers to communication between young people and their parents, and they do not speak to each other of some of the most important concerns in life.

I have the feeling that many a preacher of the gospel can recall times when he didn't get to the bedside of someone who was dying in order to once more present the gospel and God's offer of the forgiveness of sins if the person would believe on Jesus. And the preacher might feel, as you do, guilty—as if the person's eternal salvation

---

1. *The New Testament in the Language of Today* (St. Louis: Concordia, 1963).

depended altogether on a witness being given at that particular time.

Most persons have had numerous opportunities to receive Jesus Christ as Saviour. However, it is well that Christians feel an urge to once more present to a dying man or woman the message of salvation. But we ought to feel a similar urgency at other times, for all men and women are dying; all are lost without Jesus Christ as Saviour. None can be sure that he will have a tomorrow when he can accept the Saviour. For this reason God says, *"Now* is the accepted time; behold, *now* is the day of salvation" (2 Corinthians 6:2).

You cannot live in the past. You must live for the Lord in the present. Only today is yours. You must some day give an account to the Lord of how you spend today and every day until you meet Jesus face to face. You may be living in fear of that day because of the guilt you feel. But I would counsel you to remember that God is "the God of all grace," and has forgiven all your sins because of Jesus Christ who paid the debt you and I could not pay, when He died on the cross of Calvary.

What you have gone through represents a great grief for you, and only God can heal the hurt of that grief. He will do it, if you really believe in His mercy, if you really believe that He, as the righteous Judge of all the earth, will make no mistakes as He judges our lives.

Dear Frances,
I would like you to help me explain heaven to my children. They ask me about heaven and say they wish Jesus would bring my mother and father back so they could see and know them. I lost my father when I was ten years old, and my mother passed away two months before our eldest son (now sixteen years old) was born.

I know death is a graduation step and that my parents are here in spirit, but many times I have wished they were here in body to see how our children have grown.

It seems to me that you have conveyed to your children a concept of your parents as wonderful persons. Your children must feel that they have missed out on a great privilege because they haven't known their grandparents. Perhaps, too, they have heard their friends talk of visits to their grandparents' homes or of visits by their grandparents at their homes.

When your children express the wish that Jesus would bring their grandparents back to them, all you can do is explain to them that this is not in God's plan for those who die.

King David understood this, for he said, when mourning for this infant son (his son by Bathsheba), "Now he is dead, wherefore should I fast? Can I bring him back again? I shall go to him, but he shall not return to me" (2 Samuel 12:23). While the child was so seriously ill for seven days, David fasted and prayed. He prayed so earnestly then he stretched out on the earth before the Lord. But when David was told that the child was dead, he "arose from the earth, and washed, and anointed himself, and changed his apparel, and came into the house of the Lord, and *worshipped:* then he came to his own house; and when he required, they set bread before him, and he did eat" (2 Samuel 12:20).

It's interesting to note that the death of this dearly loved child became an occasion of worshiping the Lord. When a loved one is taken to heaven, it can be an occasion when you worship the Lord for His mercy in providing eternal salvation, for the home (heaven) that Jesus said He was going to prepare for His own, and for the fact that to depart and be with Christ is far better than to remain on this earth (Philippians 1:23).

The Bible records another occasion when a man who was bereaved worshiped. When Job was informed of the death of his seven sons and three daughters in one day, and of the loss of a vast amount of his possessions, Job arose, rent his mantle, shaved his head, and fell down upon the ground and worshiped. He said, "Naked came I out of my mother's womb, and naked shall I return thither: the Lord gave, and the Lord hath taken away; blessed be the name of the Lord" (Job 1:21).

Present-day believers have in the New Testament much more information about heaven than the Old Testament saints had. We know that Jesus spoke of heaven as His Father's house, a place where there are many mansions (John 14:2). Before He went to His death on the cross, He told His disciples that He was going away to prepare a place for them and that He would come again and receive them unto Himself (John 14:3). I like the clause that tells *why* He was going to do this: "that where I am, there ye may be also."

Christians sometimes talk as if the most important aspect of going to heaven is that of being reunited with their loved ones who have died believing in the Lord. But most important is the fact that we will be with Jesus our Saviour, who loved us and gave Himself for us.

God does not say that we believers in Jesus Christ shouldn't sorrow for our loved ones who have died. He knows that we become attached to those we love and the death of a loved one is for us a difficult experience—an emotional amputation, as someone has described it. It hurts. However, even though the experience of sorrow is painful, we should not sorrow as those who have no hope. This is what the apostle Paul told the Christians at Thessalonica who had experienced bereavement of loved ones who had died believing in the Lord. And he added, "Wherefore comfort one another with these words" (1 Thessalonians 4:18). What words? The words found in verses 14 to 17 of that chapter. In those verses the apostle Paul taught this: that at the return of the Lord those who had died as believers in the Lord would be brought *with* Jesus, and then living believers would be caught up together with them in the clouds to meet the Lord in the air. And Paul added, "So shall we ever be with the Lord."

I believe that the bodies of those who died believing in the Lord will be raised and reunited with their spirits at that time, and those believers who will then be living on the earth will be changed, in a moment, in the twinkling of an eye. They will not go through the experience of death, but will at that time receive their glorified bodies, bodies like the resurrection body of our Lord Jesus Christ.

Heaven will be a wonderful place—primarily because we will see God's face (Revelation 22:4) and come to know Him better than we could ever know Him while on earth. The apostle Paul said, "Now I know in part; but then shall I know even as also I am known" (1 Corinthians 13:12). In Revelation 21:3-5 is recorded the apostle John's description of heaven. He said, "I heard a great voice out of heaven saying, Behold, the tabernacle of God is with men, and he will dwell with them, and they shall be his people, and God himself shall be with them, and be their God. And God shall wipe away all tears from their eyes; and there shall be no more death, neither sorrow, nor crying, neither shall there be any more pain: for the former things are passed away. And he that sat upon the throne said, Behold, I make all things new."

And in that place where all things shall be new, we shall be occupied in serving God. We read in Revelation 22:3 that "his servants shall serve him." It's a real challenge to my imagination to think of what will be involved in that service.

Regarding your parents, you say that you know they are "here in spirit." As far as I know, there is nothing in the Bible which teaches that those who have died are present with us as disembodied spirits, observing the activities of their loved ones.

You say, "I have wished they were here in body to see how our children have grown." The period of your children's growth is but a brief segment of a life that is of short duration compared to eternity. I think it would be more appropriate for you to be concerned about your children's spirtual growth so that they may faithfully serve the Lord while on earth. Then when they appear before the Lord in heaven and receive from the Lord His rewards and commendation, "Well done, thou good and faithful servant," this will bring great joy to their grandparents and to all the family of God. If there is great joy in heaven over one sinner who repents, certainly there will be great joy in heaven over the spiritual growth and development of those who have been born into the family of God and over spiritual victories they have won.

Because I think it will be helpful, I quote a paragraph written by Robert J. Little on this subject:

> The Bible encourages, and even commands, love between members of earthly families. But we must ever be conscious of Christ as both the Source and Object of our deepest joy and blessing. Sometimes when a loved one is taken away in death, the lives of those left behind are shattered, as though Christ has no consolation sufficient to make up for the loss of a loved one. Certainly we miss them, and mourn their loss. Scripture has no criticism of this. But if Christ can satisfy our hearts only if the members of our family are included, then we are failing to give Him the place of supremacy in our hearts which He de-

serves. How then could a person find satisfaction in heaven whose family were not with him there?[1]

Dear Frances,

I hope you can help me.

Recently we lost my father-in-law. Before he died he accepted the Lord, and we are so thankful for this answer to our prayers for him.

My mother-in-law, who is a fine Christian, is having such a hard time. They were married forty years. She said she knows he is with the Lord, but she wishes they could have had a few more years when they could have loved the Lord and served Him together.

She has five married children, two of whom live out of the state. We all try to see her as much as possible. We call her three to four times a week, but every time we call, she starts to cry. It is so hard to comfort someone over the phone.

Is there anything we can do that we're not doing now? We're praying for her and the whole family. My husband is taking it hard, but he has his family, job, and church work.

Could you tell me of any books that would be of help to her?

Your letter illustrates the situation of many who want to help someone who has been bereaved. We can do everything possible to show our love—through phone calls, visits at their home, picking them up to go shopping or to see friends, and so on. But it seems none of this attention eases their grief. It takes time for the hurt of separation from a loved one to heal. And it is the bereaved person who must work through her grief and make the adjustments necessary to a new way of life. It isn't easy, but it's possible. And we who are Christians have at our

1. *Here's Your Answer* (Chicago: Moody, 1967), p. 124.

disposal more resources for facing grief than do non-Christians.

I'm glad to know that your father-in-law accepted the Lord before he died. It's natural that your mother-in-law wishes that he and she could have had a few years together for loving and serving the Lord. But perhaps it was the crisis of this last illness that caused him to feel the absolute necessity of accepting Jesus Christ as his Saviour if he were to be sure of life with God beyond this life. If this is true, she can give thanks to the Lord for the circumstances that brought him to this decision. Many people are too ill near the end of life to be able to think clearly enough to believe in Jesus Christ and to receive Him as Saviour.

Continue to stand by your mother-in-law by showing your love and being helpful, and by praying for her. Be patient with her. She is going through a most difficult experience.

The following are some books that I recommend on the subject of grief:

Beside Still Waters, by Phyllis Michael (Grand Rapids: Zondervan, 1969).

The Christian Way of Death, by Gladys Hunt (Grand Rapids: Zondervan, 1971).

Good Grief, by Granger E. Westberg (Philadelphia: Fortress, 1962).

Grief's Slow Work, by Harold Bauman (Scottdale, Pa.: Herald, 1960).

His Comfort, by Norman Harrison (Minneapolis: HIS International, n.d.).

In Grief's Lone Hour, by John M. Drescher (Scottdale, Pa.: Herald, 1971).

Managing Grief Wisely, by Stanley P. Cornils (Grand Rapids: Baker, 1967).

Not by Accident, by Isabel Fleece (Chicago: Moody, 1964).

When a Child Dies, by Joseph Bayly (Chicago: Moody, 1966).

When Death Takes a Father, by Gladys Kooiman (Grand Rapids: Baker, 1968).

When Loved Ones Are Called Home, by Herbert Wernecke (Grand Rapids: Baker, 1972).

When We Wonder Why, by John Wilder (Chicago: Moody, n.d.).

You and Your Grief, by Edgar N. Jackson (Manhasset, N.Y.: Channel, 1962).

Dear Frances,

I have a problem and would like your advice.

My sister's husband died in October, and we just found out about it at Christmas time through a letter from my brother, who lives near my sister. They live in Texas. I called my sister the same day I heard about her husband's death. Now I want to write to her.

How does one go about trying to give comfort to someone you haven't seen for ten years, when you don't know if the person who passed away was a Christian or not? Anything one might say could bring sorrow.

Please let me know. Thank you.

I think your following through on your first reaction—to call your sister—was good. In this way she learned that you had just gotten the news about her husband's death.

If I were you, I would not comment, in any note you write now, on the subject of whether her husband was a Christian. To convey doubt that he was a Christian would, as you say, only increase her sorrow.

Express your sympathy for her in her aloneness. Let her know that you are thinking of her and praying for her.

Of course, when the person who died has given during his lifetime a testimony of his faith in Jesus both by word and by life, then it is comforting to say to those who have been bereaved (if they are Christians too), "You have a precious hope of seeing your loved one again."

I can well understand that when you are uncertain about whether the deceased had personally trusted in Jesus as his Saviour, you would feel dishonest about trying to give comfort by implying that he was a Christian. It would be appropriate to say something like this: "You have many good memories of the years you shared together" and assure her that God will comfort her in her grief if she will trust in Him.

Dear Frances,

Something has been bothering me deeply, and I feel certain your Christian advice will help me to arrive at peace about the matter. Since you have been married twice, I feel you can be of help.

My mother has been married twice—eighteen years to my father and twenty-three years to her second husband. Both of them are deceased, and the problem is this: which husband will she be buried with?

I was the only child in our family and closer to my parents than children who have brothers and sisters. My father was a wonderful father, and I wish every child could have the benefit that I had because of the loving understanding I received from my father and the enjoyment of his companionship. My mother married the second time when I was twenty-three years of age, and the same year I got married. Her second husband and I always got along congenially, but I never thought of him as a father and he never thought of me as a daughter.

Both of the men to whom my mother was married had bought extra cemetery lots. When my mother's second husband died, his relatives asked where she was going to be buried. When she stated that it was her plan to be buried next to her first husband, these relatives were very much hurt and suggested that his body should have been brought to the family cemetery for burial. After that, my mother decided that she should be buried next to her second husband.

I can't possibly tell you how bad I felt about this decision, and I fought back the tears as I told my mother how I felt. I just never could feel right about burying my mother anywhere but next to my father, but I keep feeling that maybe I am childish and selfish in my feelings about this.

Well, Mother decided to be buried next to my father after all. She said her decision to be buried next to my stepfather was a mistake that she made in the past, that she couldn't dwell upon it now or in the future, and she was sure she would be forgiven. I suggested the possibility of my stepfather's body being transferred to his family's cemetery, but she said no—that it would cost too much.

Maybe the real problem is *me* and my thinking. Do you feel that my attitude is wrong? After all, I was the only child of the first marriage, and it means so much to me to have my parents laid to rest together. However, since I am emotionally involved, I find it difficult to be objective.

I agree with you that the problem is *you*. Because of your fond memories of your close relationship with your father you reacted emotionally to the decision of your mother to be buried next to your stepfather, since this decision seemed to indicate that she was giving preference to her second husband. When a woman marries a second time, this does not mean that she does not value the love and companionship she had in her first marriage. She who has loved well in her first marriage can love well in her second marriage. Her second husband does not take the place of her first husband. Her second husband has his own place in her life.

You and your stepfather's relatives have put pressure on

111

your mother concerning a decision that will not matter in the least to her once she has died and has gone to be with the Lord. Death breaks the bond of a marriage, as stated by the apostle Paul in Romans 7:2: "The woman which hath an husband is bound by law to her husband so long as he liveth; but if the husband be dead, she is loosed from the law of her husband."

Jesus' answer to the question that the Pharisees put to Him about a woman who had been married successively to seven brothers, each of whom had died, will shed some light on your problem. The Pharisees asked Jesus, "In the resurrection, whose wife will she be?" Jesus' reply indicated that marriage is a relationship that belongs to *this* world, not to the world to come. He said, "Marriage is for people here on earth, but when those who are counted worthy of being raised from the dead get to heaven, they do not marry" (Luke 20:34-35, TLB).

Your mother, while she lives on this earth, will speak of and remember her first husband and her second husband. But now that they have died, neither is her husband. To me it seems not at all important *where* she will be buried, except as she thinks of the effect of her decision on you or on her second husband's relatives.

Perhaps the best solution in such a case would be for the woman to be buried in a plot by herself. But if your mother were to make such a decision, you would feel hurt. I'm assuming this because of what you have said about your emotional reaction to the possibility of your mother's being buried anywhere except next to your father.

If I were you, I would leave matters as they are now and not disturb your mother by further talk about this matter. On the day of the resurrection of God's children, it won't matter *where* anyone is buried. What will be transcendentally important will be the great and glorious event in which all who have believed in Jesus Christ will participate. They will hear the trump of God and the voice of the Son of God, and their spirits, which had been in the presence of God since the time of their death, will be reunited with their bodies that had been in the graves of the earth. Then their redemption will be complete, and they will serve and worship the Lord in bodies that will be freed from the law of sin and death, bodies that will be freed from the limitations of physical strength and the limitations of time and space that we experience during the years of our earthly life.

And Other Sorrows

Dear Frances,

I'm wondering if you have something special to say to mothers like myself. I have two boys (five and four) who are perfectly normal and a little girl of two who is severely brain damaged. My grief, for a long time after her birth, was so extreme that I wondered how I could feel such pain and yet go on living.

There was a period of almost a year in which she made no progress and had seizures that required us to rush her to the hospital for a sedative strong enough to put her to sleep. She still has such seizures every couple of months or so. She's terribly thin, and it's a real struggle to feed her. I live in fear that each day will be her last. Yet I tell myself it would be best.

It hurts so much for me to see her rocking herself in bed, smiling only to herself and only able to squeal through clenched jaws. She has never looked at or reached for a toy and has never been able to hold her head in control.

I still grieve to see her that way. My husband says I'm displaying a lack of faith by my sorrow. My mother says that I must not wallow in self-pity. Friends have told me I should not dare to question God's wisdom in allowing my baby to be born as she was. My minister only said, "Yes, I understand; it's hard." His sympathy helped me the most of all that has been said to me. My mother-in-law says this is God's way of pun-

ishing me. My sister-in-law says I didn't eat enough
during my pregnancy.

I wonder why most people hurt instead of help me.
This I do know: God is with me, and someday I hope
to see my little girl as she was meant to be.

I certainly sympathize with you in your grief.

Sometimes those who have been bereaved of a loved
one think *their* grief is the worst grief. However, when
a loved one is taken by death, those who are left behind
can be comforted in the knowledge that his suffering is
over and in the assurance (if the loved one was a believer
in Christ) that they will see him again some day in the
presence of God in heaven. But when an infant or small
child has to suffer as your child does, this is a grief with
which you must live day after day. It would be abnormal
not to react with grief.

Sorrow doesn't imply a lack of faith. The apostle Paul,
in 1 Thessalonians 4, referred to the fact that Christians
sorrow but not as those who have no hope. Christians
do not sorrow as those do who refuse to believe that God
is a God of love and a God who always acts wisely, even
when permitting those He loves to experience grief and
pain. God certainly loved His Son, Jesus Christ, and yet
He allowed His Son to be put to grief—and to such an
extent that He was called a man of sorrows and described
as one who was acquainted with grief.

In my opinion, you are displaying faith, for faith is
confidence in God. You expressed such confidence when
you wrote, "I know that God is with me, and some day I
hope to see my little girl as she was truly meant to be."

It seems that your friends and relatives are something
like Job's friends who came to comfort him in his troubles.
They certainly failed with their philosophizing, reasoning,
and questions—so much so that Job exclaimed, "Miserable
comforters are ye all."

116

Even though friends tell you that you should not dare to question God's wisdom in allowing your baby to be born as she was, I am strongly persuaded that God understands when our hearts cry out, "Why? Why?" This heart cry represents our search for answers to the question of the ages: "Why should the righteous suffer?" And this closely related question: "Why should innocent children suffer?" There are no simple answers to these questions, for now we know in part, but then (when we see God) we shall know fully, even as we are known (see 1 Corinthians 13:12). Until that happy time, we can honor God by trusting Him and accepting His grace for our trials and His comfort for our sorrows.

Dear Frances,

My husband and I have been married for over six years and have no children. We both pray each night that if it be God's will a baby will come to bless our home. It's hard to understand and accept that perhaps it is God's will that we should be childless when so many children are being born outside of wedlock.

Can you help me with this problem?

If you and your husband have not gone to your physician for his examination of both of you, I would advise you to do this, for in recent years medical science has expanded its knowledge of how to help childless couples become parents.

If it seems unlikely that you will have a child of your own, apply to an adoption agency. Though the number of babies available for adoption is less now than in former years, you may be one of the fortunate couples who will be able to adopt a child.

Your question about why you should be childless is like some other questions in life that have no easy answers. God may allow a couple to be childless in order that they may give their love, care, and a good home to children who would not otherwise have these. Adoptive parents who have had both natural children and adopted children have told me that they find they love the adopted child as much as the natural child.

A nurse who used to live next door to me said she believed God allowed her to be childless in order that she might be free to give professional care (along with her love) to several members of her family who experienced long and serious illnesses.

Though you cannot understand why God has up until this time withheld the blessing you so much desire, you can trust Him. He is always good; He is always wise; and He has a long-range plan in view.

Dear Frances,

Several months ago I wrote to tell you that I was living in a halfway house after seven years hospitalization in a state institution. I want to thank you for answering my questions about why people are so prejudiced against those afflicted mentally in some way, such as retardation, epilepsy, and mental illness, and discriminate against them when they attempt to get jobs.

Now I would like to ask a few more questions.

The first one is this: How can a mental patient know, love, and serve God? Shouldn't we all do these things whether we are sick or well? Whether we can work or not? Even when we are idle? Even when we cannot feel His presence or love? What about those who are out of contact with reality? We all are to some degree when we are mentally ill.

Here at the halfway house we have 185 people who have been emotionally or mentally disturbed. A few are retarded, and quite a few are epileptic. Many seemingly have no faith of a religious nature, go to no church, and perhaps never pray. We are all poor;

many are on relief or dependent on family care. Some have jobs, but very few have real job security. I've seen many struggle to get well, improve somewhat, get jobs (usually poorly paid ones), struggle along for a while, get sick again, and be placed in the state hospital again. The cycle starts again and is repeated over and over. It's very discouraging to see these things happen year after year.

Many—perhaps most—cannot get jobs at all. They come and go, and come back again. The picture is pretty bleak. Sometimes everything seems so hopeless. Life seems not to be worthwhile.

Many wonder why they got sick with a mental disorder in the first place (if they realize they are sick). Many, or most, of them don't realize this.

I'm one of the luckier ones. I realize I had a breakdown, and I know how to go about overcoming it. My battle is already half or three-quarters won. Thank God, I never gave up religion or prayer, and I am finding my way. Most of those I have observed who gave up faith are not making any progress at all. See how important faith in God is?

Thank you for answering my questions.

I am glad to hear that half your battle, or three-quarters of it, is already won. I am glad to hear also what your faith in God has meant to you.

Now, before I attempt to answer your question, I want to say a few words about those individuals who have epilepsy. I do not think epilepsy should be considered a *mental* illness. At least two million persons in the United States are thought to be epileptic, and studies of thousands of persons with epilepsy have shown that normal intelligence is the rule. The late Dr. Frederick W. Stamps analyzed the records of fifty thousand patients and found little evidence of retarded mentality. He discovered only

6 percent to be less than normal intellectually. While the majority of persons with epilepsy have average intelligence, as in the general population there are brilliant exceptions—some are genius level. And, as in every group, outstanding figures who have experienced epileptic seizures have made their mark on history. Among these are Alexander the Great, Julius Caesar, Napoleon—more recently, Alfred Nobel; writers Dostoevski and de Maupassant; the painter Vincent van Gogh; the widely known baseball star, Tony Lazzeri; and a host of others both talented and capable.

Medical treatment *prevents* most seizures.

Although many people think of persons with epilepsy as handicapped, the majority are not. There are thousands of individuals now employed who successfully keep their problem secret. A fully controlled epileptic cannot be distinguished from anybody else. He appears and acts perfectly normal.

However, far too many persons with epilepsy still are victims of age-old attitudes based on ignorance, fear, and superstition. But increasing numbers of our citizens are determined to get rid of injustice and to get the facts about epilepsy known.

Now, I respond to your first question: How can a mental patient know, love, and serve God? I can't generalize, for there are so many types of mental illness. But when a person is rational he can read the Bible and can comprehend sermons, Sunday school teaching, and books which explain biblical truth. A relationship with God does not depend on great reasoning powers. Something Jesus said, as recorded in Luke 18:15-17, indicates that we need only the simplicity of faith and love of a little child to come to Jesus. Jesus said to His disciples, when they rebuked the parents who brought their children to Him to be blessed, "Let the little children come to me! Never send them away! For the Kingdom of God belongs to men who have hearts as trusting as these little children's. And anyone who doesn't have their kind of faith will never get within the Kingdom's gates" (TLB).

God is revealed in the Bible as a God of mercy and compassion. He is also a righteous God. Because of these characteristics of God, the child of God can always have confidence that the Judge of all the earth will do right (Genesis 18:25).

In reply to your question, "Shouldn't we all do these things [know, love, and serve God] whether we are sick or well, whether we can work or not?" I would say that what God values most from any individual is this: loving God when we are unable to actively serve Him. A mis-are ill and feel so weak, we can love God. We can love God when we are unable to actively serve Him. A missionary in India, Amy Carmichael, was laid aside from active missionary service for twenty years before her death. She learned what it meant to be retired from active service and to be cared for by others. She wrote, "Sometimes the only service you can render to God when you are ill is just to look up into His face and say, 'I love you.' "

I feel I am not qualified to comment on your question about those who are out of contact with reality except to say that persons who are out of touch with the real world around them have thoughts and emotions which we cannot discern. And who can tell what contact with God a person might have (a person who had previously come to faith in God, when he was well) during a period when he isn't communicating with persons around him?

Of one thing you can be sure after reading the four gospels: When God was in this world in human flesh in the person of Jesus Christ, He showed great compassion to all who suffered and through His mighty power met the needs of many who previously had been unable to find any help or cure. Today we who believe on the Lord Jesus can look to God, Who is still loving, gracious, merciful, and kind, and ask Him to undertake for our loved ones who are ill. Sometimes He will heal directly, and sometimes He will use medical means for healing, in answer to prayer. And sometimes, for reasons we cannot understand, He does not grant healing.

My mind is too puny to understand and explain the ways of God. But I can love Him and trust Him. And you can too.

In Worship and Study

Dear Frances,

I regularly listen to your "Woman to Woman" radio talks. Now I am writing to let you know that I am worrying about something at my church.

The pastor began a Bible class that I thought was going to be very good, but to my surprise it is not good at all (at least to me). He begins the class without prayer. He tells us that he doesn't believe everything in the Bible. Also, he smokes while he teaches.

Should I as a Christian be worried about these things? Please give me your view.

I can see why you would be disappointed. What is the use of studying the Bible if you do not believe it is a trustworthy record of God's dealings with men and His revelation of Himself to men? When we approach the study of the Bible believing that it is the inspired, infallible Word of God, then we can accept its teachings as a reliable guide for our faith and conduct, we can rest on the promises made by God to give comfort to Christians going through trials, and we can have hope for the future—of life after death for those who believe in Jesus Christ and of the coming of the Lord Jesus Christ to reign upon this earth, thus giving the world a period of righteousness and peace and fulfilling the prophecy of a time when "nation shall not lift up sword against nation, neither shall they learn war any more."

Referring to your remark about the pastor's beginning the class without prayer, I would say that while most periods of Bible study are begun with a prayer for God's blessing upon the teacher and the members of the class, you should not assume that the pastor did not pray before he came to the Bible class. I might mention that I do not voice a prayer on my "Woman to Woman" program, but I pray much about the selection of subjects to discuss, my preparation for the program, and the production of the program.

Concerning the pastor's smoking while he teaches, I I would feel this to be inappropriate. I have never known a pastor who smoked while teaching the Word of God. Of course, most pastors I have had contact with have been nonsmokers; they abstained from the use of tobacco because they felt this was a habit that was not pleasing to the Lord.

You cannot help but be concerned about your pastor. However, your concern should not take the form of criticizing him when talking to others but rather of speaking to him directly and praying for him.

In Ephesians 6:19-18 the apostle Paul wrote about the Christian's spiritual armor, and he instructed them, after they had put on that armor (the helmet of salvation, the breastplate of righteousness, the girdle of truth, the sandals of the preparation of the gospel of peace) to take unto them the shield of faith to quench the fiery darts of Satan, and the sword of the Spirit (the Word of God). Then they were to pray. For whom were they to pray? For all the saints, or, as J. B. Phillips translates, "all Christ's men and women." And Paul added a personal request for prayer for himself: "and for me, that utterance may be given unto me, that I may open my mouth boldly, to make known the mystery of the gospel." Time and again in his epistles Paul begged the Christians to pray for him as he preached the gospel. And every preacher of the gospel today needs the prayer support of Christians.

If you feel you cannot trust your pastor as a spiritual leader, perhaps you ought to seek a church where the pastor is one who believes the Bible is the Word of God and who provides a godly example for the people of the church.

Dear Frances,
In some religions it is taken for granted that individuals kneel when they pray, but we don't do it in our church, and so at home it seems ritualistic. Is there a reference in Scripture to kneeling in prayer?

I know of no definite command requiring Christians to kneel when they pray. However, many Christians feel that they should kneel when they pray to God because this posture expresses reverence and respect. Perhaps you recall reading in the gospels about persons who came running to Jesus and knelt before Him as they made a request of Him.

The Bible refers to various postures for prayer.

In I Kings 8:54 we read that King Solomon, after concluding his prayer on the occasion of the dedication of the temple at Jerusalem, "arose from before the altar of the Lord, from kneeling on his knees with his hands spread up to heaven." Verse 55 records that "he stood, and blessed all the congregation of Israel with a loud voice, saying, Blessed be the Lord, that hath given rest unto his people." These words were a prayer, too, for they were an ascription of praise to God. So, on this occasion Solomon prayed to God in two positions: kneeling and standing.

The apostle Paul spoke of bowing his knees unto "the Father of our Lord Jesus Christ, of whom the whole family in heaven and earth is named," following these words with his prayer for the Christians at Ephesus (Ephesians 3:14-21).

In Acts 20, where we read about the apostle Paul's farewell message to the elders of the church at Ephesus, we learn that after he had concluded his farewell message to them "he kneeled down, and prayed with them all" (verse 36).

The priests of Old Testament times commonly stood as they ministered in the tabernacle and temple.

It's interesting to note in 2 Samuel 7 that King David, praying to God after the prophet Nathan had given him God's message containing the covenant that He would make with the House of David, went in "and *sat* before the Lord," and then he talked to God in prayer.

So I have given you examples of persons who stood, kneeled, or sat while praying to the Lord. And I have no doubt that some biblical personages prayed while lying on their beds (when they were sick, or when they couldn't sleep at night).

I have heard of individuals (most of the time they have been children and young people) who get into bed, cover themselves, and then pray. It seems to me that it would be easy to fall asleep while praying after you get into bed. I recall a woman in one of our parishes who used to tell her husband, "God doesn't hear those prayers." She was referring to prayers said while lying in bed.

In our home we sit when we pray before our meals. When my sons were growing up and we had morning devotions, we used to kneel at our chairs around the breakfast table after we had read a chapter from the Bible. In my personal quiet time with the Lord, when I read the Bible, I stop to pray as I read (praying it in). Then I read some more and pray some more. I sit while I do this. But when I was much younger, I used to kneel while I read and prayed.

126

When guests in our home are about to leave, we often have prayer together. We stand and pray.

In my opinion, our posture when we pray isn't as important as *why* we pray as we do. For instance, I have read of preachers who found it easy to go to sleep when they kneeled to pray with their eyes closed and who adopted the custom of praying aloud to God as they walked back and forth in their study. The famed British preacher, Charles Haddon Spurgeon, used to pray as he walked in his secluded garden.

Most important is this: that we honor God by praying to Him—first, to worship Him, to praise Him, to adore Him, to give Him thanks for all His goodness, for all the ways in which He has shown His love; next, to present our requests to Him. He has said, "Be careful for nothing, but in every thing by prayer and supplication with thanksgiving let your requests be made known unto God" (Philippians 4:6). Then we need to pray for fellow Christians. We also need to pray for those who are not Christians, that they may come to trust the Lord Jesus as Saviour. And we need to pray for those who exercise authority over us in our government (see 1 Timothy 2:1-3) that God may guide them and give them wisdom.

Dear Frances,

Up until now I have firmly believed that the King James Version of the Bible is the only Word of God and that other versions are the devil's imitation of the Word of God. Am I mistaken in this view? I am asking you this question because I have heard you quote from versions of the Bible other than the King James Version. Why do you quote from other versions?

I quote from other versions and paraphrases when I feel such a quotation will shed additional light on the subject I am discussing.

127

I firmly believe that the sixty-six books that constitute the Bible are the Word of God. I believe that "all scripture is given by inspiration of God, and is profitable for doctrine, for reproof, for correction, for instruction in righteousness: That the man of God may be perfect, thoroughly furnished unto all good works" (2 Timothy 3:16-17).

These Scriptures were inspired of God in their original languages (Hebrew and Aramaic for the Old Testament and Greek for the New Testament). The writings which make up the Bible were completed by the end of the first century. The translation that is known as the King James Version of the Bible was not completed until 1611.

So the question arises: What shall we say about all the translations and versions of the Bible that appeared between the completion of the canon of Scripture and the publication of the King James Version? Were all these the devil's imitations of the Word of God? The King James Version is an *English* translation of the Bible; and if it were the *only* Word of God, people who do not understand English would be deprived of the Word of God until they could learn English. If your view is correct, then we would have to ask this question: Are all translations into other languages—Dutch, German, Swedish, Norwegian, French, Spanish, and so on, the devil's imitations of the Bible? The answer is no.

We can be thankful to God for the careful work done by the forty-seven scholars who were appointed by King James I of England. "The excellence of the work done is attested by the simple fact that this version has held the heart of the English-speaking world for nearly three centuries, and that no subsequent version has been able to supplant it."[1]

---

1. Merrill F. Unger, *Unger's Bible Dictionary* (Chicago: Moody, 1957), p. 1114.

Every translation of the Scriptures into a language other than the original is a version of the Scriptures. Some are more accurate than others. Later translators have had access to manuscripts that bore earlier dates and which were not available previously.

When missionaries, such as those who work with the organization known as Wycliffe Translators, seek to put the Scriptures into the languages of people whose languages have not been reduced to writing, these missionaries work most diligently to convey the truth of the biblical writings as accurately and as meaningfully as possible. There have been instances when missionaries have been unable to complete the translation of a portion of the Scriptures because they could not find words in the dialect with which they were working to express certain concepts. God's love is an example.

Dr. Merrill F. Unger says that "after the Hebrew tongue became a dead language in the second century before Christ, and still more after the spread of Christianity, translations of the Hebrew Scriptures into the prevailing languages became a necessity. Accordingly, almost every language then current had at least one version, which received ecclesiastical authority, and was used instead of the original Hebrew text.

"In the case of the New Testament, there did not for a long time exist any occasion for a translation, as the Greek language, in which it was written, was universally prevalent in the civilized world at the time of the promulgation of the Gospel. In certain provinces of the Roman empire, however, the Latin soon came into common use, especially in North Africa, and hence the old Latin and afterward the Vulgate arose. Still later the Syriac version was made for the use of the oriental Christians, to whom that language was vernacular."[2]

---

2. Ibid., p. 1147.

"The Vulgate is the popular name given to the common Latin version of the Bible which is usually attributed to the work of Jerome in the third century. For many centuries the Vulgate was the only Bible generally used; and, directly or indirectly, it is the real parent of all the vernacular versions of western Europe. The Gothic version of Ulphilas alone is independent of it. In the age of the Reformation the Vulgate was rather the guide than the source of the popular versions. That of Luther (N.T., in 1523) was the most important, and in this the Vulgate had great weight."[3]

So we see that there were a number of versions, not all of which I have mentioned, prior to the time of the completion of the King James or Authorized Version in 1611. That was over 350 years ago. Since then the English language has changed, and some words which were meaningful in 1611 are obsolete now and carry little meaning to the person who has not been brought up in a home and a church where the King James Version was used.

I might refer to a few words used in the King James Version, written in what we might call Elizabethan English, which now have a different meaning: *Conversation* meant conduct, not chatting. The word *let* in 2 Thessalonians 2:7 meant "hinder" instead of the modern opposite meaning of "permit." To a youngster reading the Bible today the word *publican* would not carry as much meaning as "tax gatherer."

The first major revision of the King James Version was undertaken in Great Britain, where a new version was completed in 1885. In America, the American Standard Version was published in 1901.

Dr. Merrill C. Tenney, in an article in *Power,* spoke of the 200,000 or more changes from the King James

---

3. Ibid., p. 1154.

Version in thirty-five well-known English translations, and added that "not more than 200 seriously affected the thought of the text." He also said that "not one of these changes affects the doctrinal teaching of the Bible as a whole."

In his opinion, "not all versions are equally acceptable, because some translators were strongly prejudiced by their theological opinions and they shaped their version to support pet theories. Some translators were not aware of all the possible meanings a certain word possessed, and so may not have chosen the most accurate meaning. Most translators, however, are conscientious, and they endeavor to translate the text as accurately and clearly as possible.

"Versions that were produced by committees of carefully chosen scholars have a more dependable and more stable overall translation of the original writings than do versions produced by one person. The latter are helpful, however, as commentaries."[4]

And I might interject that it is for that reason that I quote from some of the one-man translations, such as J. B. Phillips's *New Testament in Modern English,* Kenneth Taylor's *The Living Bible,* F. F. Bruce's *Letters of Paul,* Charles Williams's *New Testament in the Language of the People,* and Kenneth Wuest's *New Testament: An Expanded Translation.* I value the additional light they give me on the text. My use of these translations, versions, or paraphrases doesn't mean that I discredit the King James Version. It is still my favorite, for it was the text used when I was studying at the Moody Bible Institute, and it was the text I used when I memorized extensive passages of the New Testament.

Dr. Tenney also said, "No one version of the Bible fully

---

4. "An Answer for Skeptics," *Adult Power,* November 4, 1962, p. 8. By permission of Scripture Press from POWER.

satisfies all evangelical scholars. But the differences in wording do not mean that all versions are unreliable or untrue. Rather, some versions are more accurate translations of the original.

"The general agreement in sense and words in the various versions outweighs the differences. The very multitude of witnesses gives us safety, for though there is disagreement in expression, there is great unity of thought. The spiritual dynamic that is demonstrated in human lives through the use of our English translations is convincing evidence that we have in our Bible the true revelation of God."[5]

So, I do not think you need to be concerned about these versions being "the devil's imitation of the Bible." What you and I need to be concerned about is wrong interpretation of the Bible and wrong application of the Bible to our lives. Just as the devil, by quoting from the Old Testament, tempted Jesus to deviate from doing the will of God, so he may tempt us to depart from God's will through wrong interpretation of Scripture when applying it to our lives.

---

5. Ibid.

Concerning Christian Service

Dear Frances,

I'm a mother of five boys, ages nine to sixteen. They have all professed to be saved, although they seldom act like it. I keep praying that the Lord will become more real to them.

I teach a Sunday school class of four- and five-year-olds and love every minute of it. I also help with vacation Bible school each year. Outside of helping a neighbor when there is need of my help, this is the full extent of my Christian service. However, I feel that I should serve the Lord more than I do, for there is so much to be done. I keep praying that the Lord would show me what He wants me to do, but so far nothing has opened to me.

I sometimes wonder if the Lord isn't trying to tell me that raising a family and helping at church is the extent of the service He expects from me. Then I think of all the needs of our country, and once again feel I should be doing more. At times I feel guilty about enjoying myself in my leisure time when there are so many unhappy people in the world.

Can you suggest some things I could do to serve the Lord while staying at home with my family?

As a Christian woman you *are* serving the Lord in your roles of homemaker, wife, and mother of five boys the ages of yours. Yours is no small job! You are doing quite a bit for the Lord by fulfilling your home responsibilities and serving at your church in the ways you describe.

You can view time taken for Bible study and prayer as contributing to your service for the Lord, for these are necessary for your spiritual growth. Be careful lest you take on too much activity and do not grow as a Christian. The kind of Christian person you are will greatly influence the lives of your boys during their growing-up years and as they go into their teen years and begin making their own decisions.

You could open your home for a child evangelism class, or you could teach such a class at someone else's home.

You could invite your neighbors to your home for a weekly Bible study. If you feel you couldn't teach on an adult level, you might ask someone else to teach. Of you could emphasize that the Bible study is to be a discussion. You, of course, would be the leader if no one else wants to do it. Being a leader requires, of course, that you study thoroughly the chapter to be discussed.

Don't minimize intercessory prayer on behalf of your pastor, missionaries you know, your unsaved neighbors, your sons, and your husband. A ministry of intercession is a hidden service for God and takes time. But, according to the apostle James, it is a highly effective ministry. He said, "The . . . prayer of a righteous man [or woman] availeth much" (James 5:16).

I would advise you to dismiss those feelings of guilt that come over you when you are enjoying a time of leisure. Every busy person needs times of relaxation. Jesus realized this. He said to His disciples after a particularly strenuous period of preaching and healing, "Let's get away from the crowds for a while and rest" (Mark 6:31, TLB).

I think parents need to see the importance of taking time to do things with their children—to go on picnics, go swimming, take trips, and attend athletic events. Too many children of Christian parents have said, looking back on their years in the parental home, "My folks were always busy in church work, and they seldom took time to have fun with us." Since bringing up a family is an important service for the Lord, I would recommend that you put more thought into how you and your husband can use your leisure time for building good family relationships, thus contributing to the emotional security of your children.

Another important responsibility of a Christian wife is that of nurturing her relationship with her husband. She ought not to become so absorbed in her children and her church work that she neglects giving time to her husband as his companion.

What God expects of each Christian is faithfulness in the place where God has set him. Faithfulness in a small place often opens opportunities to serve the Lord in a larger way.

Refuse to allow the total needs of the world to overwhelm you. Some women get so overwhelmed by the staggering needs they read about that they fail to do something about needs almost under their noses. I remember hearing a Chinese woman doctor who could have served the Lord in a number of needy places say, "The needs are so many, and I am only *one*. But what I can do I will do, by the help of God."

Dear Frances,

My husband and I are at present going through a period of questioning and concern about the matter of God's call to the mission field. We seem to have difficulty in ascertaining God's will.

When we were married, my husband planned to be a chemist; but after being discharged from military service he felt called to full-time Christian service. It seemed to both of us that the Lord was leading in this direction, so he went to a theological seminary. I am deeply grateful to the Lord for those years, as we learned much about ourselves.

However, when my husband applied for a particular field of missionary service in Europe, to which we felt led, we were turned down by both of the boards to which we applied. . . .

I feel extremely inadequate for the role of a pastor's wife or a missionary wife since I am shy, slow-moving, not a good leader. I can scarcely believe God would call me to a role so alien to my personality. Yet I am aware that Moses underestimated his ability—or rather, God's ability to use him.

My husband was an assistant pastor for one year and began to see that he has a communication problem. Some have said he is brusque. He is very brilliant and creative but often gives the impression he is not listening to others, which communicates to them that he doesn't care. This is a serious problem for a pastor or missionary or anyone who feels called to work with people. He does not preach well (perhaps this is because of lack of opportunity), but he is a very good teacher. He is mechanically inclined and has always loved math.

The apparent closing of the door to the mission field has stunned my husband. Our families, who were impressed before (I guess), have acted as if he were a failure.

He has found a secular job, and we are making a home and waiting to see what God will do with us. We do not want to step ahead of Him. It seems He is pleased to have us wait.

I am thankful that I have been given insight from the Lord as to our problems. But my poor husband is so depressed by what has happened plus the responsibility of a family of five to care for and the realization that he is now thirty and growing older.

What is God's will? We don't know. There seem to be
no doors to knock on, so we just go about the ordinary
pursuits of life (job, home, and family) and wait for
God to interrupt as He did with Moses, Samuel, David,
Abraham, Jacob, and so on. What else is there to do?
   Will you pray for us? We are so confused right now.
. . . Sometimes when we are tired, doubts flood in—
and fear that perhaps we are all wrong and being
punished for something.

I have prayed for you, that God may lead you out of
confusion into an understanding of His will. He has said
in His word, "Be ye not unwise, but understanding what
the will of the Lord is" (Ephesians 5:17). I am strongly
persuaded that God is not so unreasonable as to expect
us to do His will if it were impossible for us to know
what His will is.

First of all, we can understand what God's will is as far
as the general principles for living the Christian life are
concerned. We find these principles as we read the New
Testament.

But what about specific leading? I believe that God will
not leave us in the dark if we sincerely want to know and
do His will. Jesus said, "If any man will do his will [God's
will], he shall know of the doctrine" (John 7:17).

Jesus also said, "I am the light of the world: he that
followeth me shall not walk in darkness, but shall have
the light of life" (John 8:12). Followers of Christ need
not be confused. You can know that you are walking
in fellowship with God, and you can be confident that
His specific will will ultimately be made known to you.
Since men and women are among God's most precious
resources, He will want to use you and your husband in
some way.

God knows what He wants you to do. He makes no
mistakes in leading us, but it is the imperfect and in-

competent human instrument who tends to make mistakes in determining God's will and in carrying out God's will in his life.

One way that God guides us is through our circumstances and our capabilities.

Circumstances would include doors that are shut. You experienced the shutting of doors to service in the particular country to which you wanted to go when two different mission boards failed to accept you as missionaries.

When these boards said no to your application, was it because they didn't need you on a particular field? Sometimes a person thinks of God's call to serve Him as a geographical call—a call to a particular location. In my opinion, it is better to commit yourself to the Lord to serve Him wherever He opens a door for you. Then when you apply to a particular missionary organization, you will allow them to designate where you will be located. Of course, this means that you will be praying that God will guide and direct the board members in their decisions.

When these boards did not accept you, it may have been that they saw in you or your husband some personality characteristics that they felt were undesirable, or they may have seen that you lacked some qualities which they felt were necessary for an appointee under their board.

I have served on the candidate committee of a missionary board, so I know how the candidate committee members and the members of the board as a whole wrestle over some decisions. When they decide to say no to a person's application because he doesn't meet their qualifications, they realize how difficult it will be for the applicant who wants very much to serve the Lord to accept their decision. But if they send to the field one who will in all likelihood be a failure, in their judgment, this will be a waste of money given for missions and a waste of three, four, or five years of the applicant's life before he gets settled in the work the Lord wants him to do.

From your letter I can tell that you see some of your deficiencies and some of your husband's deficiencies. These, plus the denial of your applications for missionary service, may be taken as indications of the Lord's leading.

You refer to God's dealing with Moses. Even though God told Moses, who seemed to be lacking in eloquence, that He would be with his mouth and teach him what he should say, this doesn't mean that God will say that same thing to every man who is slow of speech and has difficulty in communicating. God said that to *Moses*. Even so, Moses demurred. In response, God told Moses he should speak God's words to Aaron, and then Aaron should be Moses' spokesman to the people of Israel.

We can find encouragement in the Bible from the examples of the kind of individuals God used as His servants, but I think we need to exercise discernment when we think of applying His promises to them to ourselves when we are seeking guidance for ourselves.

In my opinion, each person needs to have an *inner certainty* of God's guidance. God's guidance will take into consideration the individual's willingness to do God's will (whatever that will may be), his natural gifts with which God endowed him and which can be developed by training, and circumstances.

If God seems to be shutting doors to what is called full-time Christian service, it is no disgrace to serve Him in a secular vocation, in your home life, in bringing up your children for the Lord, and in a local church as laymen. In fact, this is the way most Christians serve the Lord. Even though you aren't in full-time Christian work, you are a Christian full time, and you can faithfully and joyfully serve the Lord in the ways I have mentioned.

I realize that what has happened is hard on your husband's family, if they had fondly hoped to see him serving God as a missionary or a pastor. But don't worry about that. Perhaps their pride has been hurt, since their son will not have the prestige attached to being a missionary or a pastor. But the important thing is for you and your husband to recognize whether you have reached for service beyond your capabilities. If this should be true, then you will need to learn to be content with serving the Lord in some other way.

As you and your husband think about his vocation, it would be well for you to ponder this concept: God draws no line between the secular and the sacred.

If your husband's aptitudes can best be used in a secular job (perhaps as a teacher), he can be God's servant in that capacity. He can keep in mind the admonition, "Whatsoever ye do in word or deed, do all in the name of the Lord Jesus, giving thanks to God and the Father by him" (Colossians 3:17). A Christian in a secular job is often used of God to witness to persons who might never be reached by a pastor or missionary.

While Jesus said to His disciples, "Go ye into all the world, and preach the gospel" (Mark 16:15), for some of us the world into which we can go and preach the gospel is the world where we work and live. We can all *be* witnesses even though we haven't been commissioned to service as a missionary or ordained as a pastor. As someone has said, "Missions begins when the sinner crosses your path."

Dear Frances,

In my twenty-eight years as a pastor's wife, I have felt deprived of the privilege of having a real friend in whom I can freely confide. I am nearly always "on guard." How have you handled the delicate problem of close relationships in your experience as a pastor's wife?

I think many a pastor's wife starts out in her husband's first pastorate with an apprehensive feeling about close friendships. She feels like a person who is walking on eggs. She is on guard because she has heard so much about manifestations of jealousy and envy if the pastor and his wife relate more closely to some members of their congregation than they do to others.

It's part of our humanity that we desire close friends— friends who are loyal, friends in whom we have confidence and in whom, therefore, we can confide. In my experience I found it best to have such friends outside of the congregation to which my husband was ministering. He and I tried to treat all members of the congregation alike, though I must admit that it wasn't easy, for some people attract you more than others and are more outgoing and expressive of their affection, wanting to do things for you that express their love. You must be alert to the possibility of becoming obligated to those who express their feeling toward you with gifts and of feeling that they should be given special consideration in decisions related to church activities.

It may be part of the price of serving God effectively to have to do without the close friendships for which you long—that is, within the membership of your congregation. But God is able to give you some compensations. I have found this to be true. For instance, a pastor's wife has a closer relationship with her husband and his work than does the wife of a man in most other occupations. And when you move to a new location, you are automatically provided with a group of people who are interested in you and want to know you, and who will show you many kindnesses, even though you will not allow yourself to become involved in close friendships with them—the kind in which you "let down your hair." Be thankful for blessings such as these.

I would suggest that you try to find some couple in your town from another church with whom you can get together frequently. It may be that you will find a couple living in another town, with whom you can have spiritual fellowship and opportunities for relaxation. My husband and I and our three sons, as they were growing up, got together every week or so (usually on a Saturday) with a couple with three children who lived in a city thirty miles away. During the summertime we met for picnics at a beach, during the fall at a park where the men and boys played touch football, followed by a picnic dinner. During the winter months we alternated going to each other's homes on Saturdays for dinner and a few hours of games such as pingpong, box hockey, or table games in which all participated. And during the hours of meal preparation and clearing up later, my friend and I engaged in the kind of conversation women enjoy so much, a sharing of the things that interested us, the concerns on our hearts, our aspirations and hopes for our children.